TAKE IT FROM ME

Celebrities share practical, inspiring, and witty secrets of success in this winning collection!

If one is lucky, a solitary fantasy can totally transform one million realities.
—Maya Angelou

Watch which laws you break.
—Heidi Fleiss

What's money? A man is a success if he gets up in the morning and gets to bed at night and in between he does what he wants to.
—Bob Dylan

Eighty percent of success is showing up.
—Woody Allen

If you want something said, ask a man. If you want something done, ask a woman.
—Margaret Thatcher

The secret to success is to learn to accept the impossible, to do without the indispensable, and bear the intolerable.
—Nelson Mandela

If you want the rainbow, you gotta put up with the rain.
—Dolly Parton

TAKE IT
FROM ME

Practical and Inspiring Career Advice
from the Celebrated and the Successful

Michael Levine

A Perigee Book

Kind permission has been granted to reprint the following:

Excerpt appearing on pages 126–127 from *The Employee Handbook of New Work Habits for a Radically Changing World: 13 Ground Rules for Job Success in the Information Age* by Price Pritchett, © 1994 by Price Pritchett. Published by Pritchett & Associates, Inc., Dallas, TX.

Excerpt appearing on pages 130–133 adapted from *The Art of War for Women* by Judith Regan, Crown Books, 1996.

Excerpt appearing on pages 84–85 by Fred Rogers, © 1995 by Family Communications, Inc.

A Perigee Book
Published by The Berkley Publishing Group
200 Madison Avenue
New York, NY 10016

Copyright © 1996 by Michael Levine
Book design by Rhea Braunstein Design
Cover design by James R. Harris

First edition: June 1996

Published simultaneously in Canada

The Putnam Berkley World Wide Web site address is
http://www.berkley.com

Library of Congress Cataloging-in-Publication Data

Library of Congress Cataloging-in-Publication Data
Take it from me : practical and inspiring career advice from the
   celebrated and the successful / [compiled by] Michael Levine.—
   1st ed.
        p.   cm.
      "A Perigee book."
      Includes index.
      ISBN 0-399-52217-4
      1. Vocational guidance—Quotations, maxims, etc.   2. Career
development—Quotations, maxims, etc.   I. Levine, Michael.
HF5381.T2216   1996   95-26809
650.1—dc20   CIP

PRINTED IN THE UNITED STATES OF AMERICA

10   9   8   7   6   5   4   3   2   1

Contents

Foreword

A close friend recently said to me, "I hope your new book sells a ton." I replied, "It doesn't matter. I'm pleased with it."

Of course I hope my new book sells a ton! But the only quality control monitor who counts in the end is me.

Or you: Have you done your best (at whatever, inconsequential or monumental)? Have you stretched yourself to the breaking point? Have you had a ball, made an idiot out of yourself, and learned something in the process? *Are you proud of the result?*

The sages say "the journey is the reward." They are right! Putting your whole self *into* a task, engaging, stoking your curiosity at every turn, developing passion, commitment and camaraderie in conjunction with your teammates. Those are the highs you look back on.

The life lived fully—with spirit and flair and care—that's the ticket. The "bottom line" (fame, fortune, etc.) can be very modest or very immodest. (We often confuse the two. The so-called "modest"—raising a child, helping just one troubled teenager—are the most immodest of "successes.") It's your ability to smile (or better yet grin) when you see your face in the morning that ultimately counts.

Tom Peters, businessman, author of
the best-selling book
In Search of Excellence

Introduction

Take it From Me is an inspiring and excellent collection of career advice. It incorporates the original thoughts and ideas of some of the most successful men and women of our time—their wisdom, ideas, and encouragement. I suggest that it be read in the same way it was assembled—a little at a time. Some of the ideas that seem most simple actually have tremendous depth and power if you think deeply about them.

In some ways this book could be added to the mountainous pile of books that already exists on the topic of success. It's a subject that has been studied and written about to the point of saturation squared. But this book is about more than just success. About halfway through the compilation process, it occurred to me that while success may be examined carefully, its opposite, failure, has not been written about enough. Strange. For doesn't it make sense that if there are secrets to success there certainly must be secrets to failure. You will see, however, especially in the section "If at First You Don't Succeed . . . ," that failure was the very key to success for many.

I should present my credentials. I attended college for six months, quit, and have been self-employed ever since. With that background, no one was more surprised than me to be invited a few years back to speak at Harvard Business School. It was a fascinating experience, putting me face-to-face with America's "best and brightest." I had lots to say that day, and decided to end my speech with a version of George Orwell's comment that "some ideas are so stupid only intellectuals can believe them." One of the points I was trying to make with that remark was that at the core of career advice are elements that are pure common sense; they don't require advanced degrees or book learning. You'll see examples of that in this book over and over again. Many keys to success may seem obvious, but are tragically overlooked or forgotten.

There are more than a few themes that run throughout the book that bear touching on here:

- Success requires energy. In fact, it eats it for breakfast. Most at the top of their game have a ton of energy and use it well. They seem to have been in another line when God was handing out patience, and have great difficulty understanding procrastination.
- Good ideas are common. The people who implement them are rare.
- Passion. Inexpressibly important.
- Imagination. The ability to envision alternative scenarios.

- Self-determination. Winners act out of choice. They are never victims of fate.

Studies show that winning factors also include focus, toughness, persistence and, yes, instinct over intellect.

The subject that interests me most is attitude. While researching his book *Wealth and Poverty,* George Gilder wanted to know why some people come from nowhere and succeed brilliantly, while others seem to lose their way. He talked to scores of criminals in prison, and nearly all of them have the same theories of economic success: All wealth, in their opinion, comes from stealing: successful Italian restaurants are fronts for organized crime; successful actresses, models and businesswomen prostitute themselves; oil tycoon John D. Rockefeller, one man told Gilder, made his fortune as a member of Jesse James's gang and founded Standard Oil as a front. Gilder's interviewees explained they were merely trying to follow the same dishonest path, and were unlucky enough to get caught. In believing these silly and sad myths, these people left no room in their minds for the first rule of success: You alone are responsible for bringing it about.

I am grateful to each and every one of the prominent people who contributed original material for *Take It From Me.* Other words of wisdom contained here I discovered along the way in magazines and newspapers, on television, in interviews, and in books that fit the theme of this book so well that they needed to be included also.

In reading, and hopefully applying, the ultimate career

advice contained in this book from some of the world's most successful people, you have taken an important first step on your own path to success.

Michael Levine

Los Angeles

TAKE IT
FROM ME

1

Secrets of Success and No Fear of Failure

I have learned that in order to increase the number of my successes, I have had to accept an increase in the number of my failures. I think any success worth having is like a hundred-rung ladder. There's no use trying to jump in the middle; take it as a bottom-to-top proposition, one step at a time. Yes, to the faint of heart each of the ninety-nine of those steps represents a failure of sorts. But to those with the determination to stay the course, success is inevitable.

—Harvey MacKay, executive, business
writer, author of *Swim with the Sharks
Without Being Eaten Alive*

The single greatest thing I've learned from studying successful job hunters (and career changes) for twenty-five years is that the essence of successful job-hunting is having alternatives. Alternative ways of describing what you do. Alternative avenues of job-hunting. Alternative leads to a job. Alternative target organizations that you're going after. Alternative ways of approaching employers. The problem with unsuccessful job hunters is that they often pursue a plan that has no alternative. You must not follow in their footsteps if you want your job hunt to be successful.

—Richard Nelson Bolles, author of
What Color Is Your Parachute?

Today's career anxiety may be tomorrow's freedom to experiment. We may be on the verge of new definitions of success. Comfort with ambiguity may become a sought-after professional characteristic.

—Judy B. Rosener, professor, Graduate School of UC Irvine, author of *America's Competitive Secret: Utilizing Women as a Management Strategy*

There are no guarantees of success in life, but I've found five golden rules that can help you get where you want to go:

2

Rule One—Invest in yourself. The smartest investment you can make is to build your own asset base—the skills and capabilities that come with further education and experience. Accumulating capital will help you more than you think.

Rule Two—Demand the best from yourself in everything you do. Keep asking, "How could I have done this better?" We all fall short of perfection, but if you shoot for 100 percent, you'll get 80 percent and be far ahead of the rest of the pack.

Rule Three—Learn from your mistakes. You'll make plenty of them; we all do. But mistakes can be valuable learning experiences if you analyze why they happened and how you might have avoided them. Each mistake is a learning experience.

Rule Four—Be flexible. My own career was forever changed for the better because of incidents I could never have anticipated. So don't stick too rigidly to a career plan; leave yourself open to opportunities that will arise, and be prepared for them. Take advantage of accidents.

Finally, Rule Five—Get involved. Be multidimensional. Your career can only be enhanced by taking an active part in political and community life, and by communication with your family and associates.

>—Dwayne O. Andreas,
>Chairman of the Board/CEO,
>Archer Daniels Midland Company

I can't imagine a person becoming a success who doesn't give this game of life everything he's got.

>—Walter Cronkite,
>journalist/news reporter

Whether they be young or old, rich or poor, tall or short, the thought of advising anyone about anything fills me with dread. However, there may be one sentence I've read which might be helpful not only with career, but with life itself. It was, "Happiness consists of minimizing both our triumphs and our failures." So, my friends, if this works for you, tell 'em where you got it!

>—John Forsythe, actor

There is no greater skill to help position you for success than the ability to speak. There are many times that you will have less time to speak than you planned, be it a sales presentation, running a staff meeting or giving a talk. These tips will help you: (1) Stick to your most important point, and be confident that you can communicate it in five minutes. Do not apologize or mention that you originally had more time. (2) Begin fast by using a startling statement such as "This audience will not be the same five years from now." Follow this with a strong statement: "The number-one piece of advice I can give you today is . . ." (3) Illustrate this piece of advice with a story so that the audience can "see" it. (4) Make sure your speech has a problem and a payoff; then follow with your point of view.

—Patricia Fripp, CPAE, professional
speaker from San Francisco, author of
Get What You Want, past president of
the National Speakers Association

There is no such thing as failure—only people who quit.
—Phyllis Diller, comedienne

There is a pattern I have noticed, in my own life and in others, that seems to work out well. People with strong father figures, people who admire their fathers or are afraid of them (or both), will do for a living what their fathers did as a hobby. It enables them to follow in their father's footsteps and endorse his value system without having to compete with him directly. They sense that if they went into the same line of work that their father was in, one of two bad things would happen. They would either be less successful than he was, or they would be more successful, and they foresee problems either way. But if they do professionally what their father "played" at, entering the clergy because their father was active in their church or synagogue (as I did), becoming a therapist or lawyer because their father was a man people turned to for advice, there would be no sense of "outdoing" the father because, after all, you had professional training and all day long to do it.

—Rabbi Harold S. Kushner, author of
When Bad Things Happen to Good People

Stand your ground. It will be worth it! Accept that all of us can be hurt, that all of us can—and surely will at times—fail. Other vulnerabilities, like being embarrassed or risking love, can be terrifying too. I think we should follow a simple rule: if we can take the worst, take the risk.

—Joyce D. Brothers, Ph.D., psychologist,
syndicated columnist

How to be successful as an elected public official? Interesting question. In some ways the advice is the same as the counsel one would give for any field of endeavor. Learn all you can about whatever craft, business or profession has been chosen, and follow Polonius's classic advice to his son: "This above all, to thine own self be true, and it must follow as night the day, thou canst not be false to any man." Specifically, know your constituents and your district; learn parliamentary procedure; keep in close touch with your people and the various social, religious and business organizations that represent them; be available to them; work and speak for their interests and last, but of major importance, make regular reports in order to be certain that they are aware of your efforts.

—Jose E. Serrano, Member of Congress,
16th District, New York

Success breeds success—once you've had a good night, you can't wait to do the next night. Initial success causes you to be even more confident, pleased with yourself the next time around.

—Ed McMahon, television personality

Success is that old ABC—ability, breaks, and courage.

—Charles Luckman, architect

Always give your best and a little bit more from the very beginning of your work life. You will be surprised at the recommendations and elevated hirings that follow through your career.

—Pete Rozelle, former NFL Commissioner

The secret of any business success is to understand the customers' problems and to provide solutions so as to help them be profitable and feel good about the transaction.

—Francis G. "Buck" Rogers,
former IBM executive

There are a lot of factors that go into success. But I think one of the most important is treating other people with respect. Throughout my career I've found that the most successful businesspeople are those that never forget that business is not just about the bottom line—it's about people.

—Michael J. Roarty,
Executive Vice President,
Anheuser-Busch Companies, Inc.

One of the most important needs in the world today is to gain a new perspective concerning success and failure. It is only by superficial standards that we have come to judge greatness in terms of being served rather than of rendering service. Jobs are often judged not in terms of what is accomplished or whether they are constructive, but in terms of hours, wages and ease. Even people are judged by their ability to take from life, not give to life.

—Spencer Robinson, Jr.,
General Secretary, Rotary International

A fundamental factor in the definition of success lies in one's own evaluation of the quality of choices one has made. Without a quality education, there are no choices. Life simply "happens" and the consequences are, at best, painfully less than they could have been, and invariably, someone else's fault.

—Peter M. Palermo,
Vice President/General Manager,
Eastman Kodak Company

I don't know the key to success, but the key to failure is trying to please everybody.

—Bill Cosby, actor, comedian

I have always believed that it's important to show a new look periodically. Predictability can lead to failure. Unfortunately, I've had my share of setbacks in life, and I don't like to think back on them. Instead, I prefer focusing on the opportunities ahead.

—T. Boone Pickens, President,
Mesa Petroleum Company

Take educated risks? Make mistakes? Yes, indeed. I've always believed that the best work culture regards risk taking. It's a culture in which people have the right to be wrong and it's okay to make a mistake. But when you make a mistake, make sure you can identify it to someone else, talk to them about it, and put the appropriate resources into correcting it. Secondly, learn from your experience and don't make the same mistake again.

—Jerre Stead, President, AT&T

I began my business seventeen year ago as one of the pioneers of the direct response business in cosmetics and have learned just as much about myself as I have about the industry. The Tova Corporation specializes in skin care, hair care, fragrances and cosmetics, and was fortunate enough to get involved with the QVC Shopping Network five years ago. We have added CVC, QVC's sister network in Mexico and QVC London, making the Tova Corporation the only self-owned cosmetic company to sell its products worldwide. Both have been extremely successful and worthwhile ventures. The best advice I can give to those that are true entrepreneurs is that you must *love* what you are doing. The clearer you are about your goals, the easier the journey will be. Passion, Perseverance and Patience, this above all else is my advice. Give up the attachment to the end result and enjoy the journey that takes you to your ultimate success.

Most often those that pursue their dreams get so caught up in the outcome that they forget to enjoy the process of learning, experience and growth. Success and Failure are truly one and the same. And above anything else, always believe that It Can Be Done!

—Tova Borgnine, President/CEO,
the Tova Corporation

A challenge is the dividing line between winners and losers. Losers stay on the side of the line that figures the challenge is too big. Winners meet a challenge and go through it, over it, or around it. Keep in mind, challenges guard all success. If you want the rewards, don't quit. Keep working and get better at what you do. And don't leave them any option in the future!

—Will Clark, San Francisco Giants

To succeed, it is necessary to accept the world as it is and rise above it.

—Michael Korda, publishing executive,
Simon & Schuster, author of
The Immortals

The secret to success is to learn to accept the impossible, to do without the indispensable, and bear the intolerable.

—Nelson Mandela,
President of South Africa

Perseverance and tenacity are the two greatest ingredients to success. You can't ever give up or give in; when you fall or fail you will learn more. It will strengthen you as a person and as a worker. Success is not a goal in and of itself. After all, what is success? To me it's one thing. To a brilliant scientist it's another. To a mother it's something else again. Success is a movable goal. Once we reach one of our goals, enjoy it . . . then move on. Keep stretching, keep growing, keep learning. Life has no shortcuts. We learn by doing, by challenging ourselves, by opening ourselves to change. Change can be, and sometimes is, frightening. But when you learn to deal with your fears, face them, stand your ground, then you can truly taste success. Build alliances, care for your supportive friends and associates, don't "use" people and give nothing back. Life is full of circles, business is full of cycles, and they all blend seamlessly together. Good luck for your success.

—Ivana M. Trump, entrepreneur

The most important life lesson I can share with others is this: Success is open to anyone—if you really want it, you can have it. Success and achievement are two different things. Achievement depends on more than your own individual talents and preparedness. It also depends heavily on timing and opportunity. For opportunity we have to rely on others to give us a chance to work on even bigger canvases in our chosen fields. Successful people have a purpose in life and hunger to live a meaningful life. Successful people are able to distinguish the difference between what they have and what they are. A wise man said, "Some men and women make the world better just by being the kind of people they are."

> —R. J. Ventres, former Chairman/CEO,
> Borden, Inc.

The only thing harder to handle than winning too much is losing too much.

> —John Wooden, former basketball coach,
> UCLA, author of *They Call Me Coach*

You may be disappointed if you fail, but you are doomed if you don't try.

—Beverly Sills, opera singer

The only place where success comes before work is in the dictionary.

—Vidal Sassoon, hairstylist

Rejection is a reality in almost any undertaking that's worthwhile and it's always disappointing. However, rejection doesn't mean you can't or you won't; it simply means you're not yet ready. Like the puny little third grader, you haven't grown enough yet. You've got more work to do, more to learn.

—Gene Perret, comedy writer

Success in any organization requires remarkably similar attributes. Often, when asked by those beginning or continuing a career, I suggest five focus areas for individuals who seek advancement and increased responsibility. *Aim high*: Don't be afraid to set lofty goals. Although often over-looked, aggressive goal-setting is the key to meaningful per-sonal and business success. *Be flexible*: Obviously, our social and business environments are changing at an ever-increasing pace. Being flexible enables us to profit from change, not succumb to it. *Continuously improve*: Adopt an attitude whereby the status quo is merely a jumping-off point. Remember that if you keep on doing what you have always done, you will only get what you have always gotten. *Accept it*: Be willing to give purpose to and then set direction for the individuals with whom you become associated. This is the toughest and yet the most rewarding activity you will experience. *Achieve balance*: Establish a proper balance be-tween your personal and business lives. Each must receive constant attention. To actually succeed and have the sta-mina for maintaining that success one must not neglect one "life" for the other.

—Dr. Ray R. Irani, Chairman of the Board, President and CEO, Occidental Petroleum Corporation

To achieve success you need firm beliefs. I firmly believe that any person in order to survive and achieve success must have a sound set of beliefs on which he premises all actions.

—H. Wayne Huizenga,
CEO, Blockbuster Entertainment

As with most of life's more challenging and worthwhile pursuits, there is no easy shortcut or formula for achieving career success. When I graduated from college in 1953 and joined Reynolds, my goals were to work hard, do the very best job possible and learn from the experience. They seem simple but over the years I have come to the realization that these goals are not easily, if ever, attained. Today, as company chairman, I still approach my work with the same standards in mind that I set for myself forty-one years ago as a sales trainee. My advice to those embarking on a career would be to avoid the pitfalls of measuring success only in financial terms or hierarchical status. People who are fortunate enough to pursue careers where they can contribute to an organization or effort by working together with others toward a common goal will have achieved the ultimate in career success: job satisfaction and a sense of self-worth. I have found that individuals who are enthusiastic about their work and life, have ambition and determination, char-

acter and integrity, and the ability to work with others toward shared goals will succeed in any field they choose.
—Richard G. Holder, Chairman/CEO,
Reynolds Metals Company

Life is filled with successes and failures. If one can ride this roller coaster without pain and frustration, one can win out at the end. No matter what course you take in life, you will, somewhere along the road, meet with rejection. The key is to "never take rejection as the last word." I cannot tell you how many times I was rebuffed at meetings or auditions. One person didn't like my name, another my nose and another my Canadian accent. I kept all three and succeeded. There are three elements to success. The first is talent. The second is desire. And the third is luck or opportunity or fate. There is the moment when your talent and your desire meet up with the right opportunity. Stick it out until that fateful moment and you will win. Branch Rickey, the famous general manager of the old Brooklyn Dodgers, used to say that "luck is the residue of design." He might have said "the residue of desire," for it is a combination of talent and courage (pluck) that will keep you in the fight, until that "lucky" day when someone recognizes your talent.
—Monty Hall, television game-show host

What's money? A man is a success if he gets up in the morning and gets to bed at night and in between he does what he wants to.

—Bob Dylan, singer/songwriter

My only advice would be to think of success in personal terms and not be constrained by narrow prevailing notions of success which may limit you. Identify a legitimate set of goals that have meaning for you, then pursue them with determination and integrity.

—Bob Costas, NBC sports broadcaster

There are important steps young people can take to prepare themselves for a successful career. First—and probably the most important—get as much education as possible. Second, get experience. Entry level jobs are a good chance for you to get your foot in the door and work your way up the career ladder. It's also important that you set goals for yourself. Throughout your educational and professional career, plan ahead and decide where you want to be in five or ten years. Finally, be flexible, but stick to your principles. That might sound somewhat contradictory, but in real life you may need to refocus your career goals if unexpected events should occur. At the same time, you need a core of beliefs or principles that serve as a guide in your decision making process.

—Ben Cardin, Member of Congress,
3rd District, Maryland

The definition of a successful life must include serving others.

—George Bush, former United States
President

You can do it, you can succeed, you can achieve, but you must be prepared. You have to pay the price.

—Frank Borman, Commander, Apollo 8
mission, business leader

I have always grown from my problems and the challenges, from the things that don't work out, that's when I've really learned.

—Carol Burnett, actress

Eighty percent of success is showing up.

—Woody Allen, actor/writer/director

How to be successful, of course, depends largely on what the word "success" entails for each individual. For some—indeed, for most—"success" will mean financial success, and that is nothing to be sneezed at. Freedom from worry, security for one's family and a wider range of choices for one's children—these are worthy reasons to hope for success. However, my advice for the person who wants a truly satisfying career on its own terms—especially the person who is somewhat unencumbered with other obligations—is "take a chance." There is, in my opinion, *nothing* more rewarding than writing, sculpting, building, buying, acting, exactly what you choose to, rather than what it might be more sensible to. Having one's say is a tremendously therapeutic exercise—if it can be done as part of a career, I think the psychological rewards are about trebled. I also believe that success, even in the purely financial sense, does frequently come to the bold, to the chance-takers. So, if there is something offbeat, oddball, unusual that you have always wanted to turn your hand to—I would say, take a chance and do it. Success will likely come on the mental and spiritual level, and the odds that it might even come in

the financial area are much greater than you think.
—Cleveland Amory, writer

My advice is to choose a career that you are passionate about. Some people can be motivated by the sheer desire for money or power. Most require passion as well. If your work can draw upon the passion that a hobby would—and you can derive pleasure from its pursuit—you have the ingredients for a "happy marriage." Further, there is no substitute for preparation, hard work and homework. It's the old Boy Scout motto: "Be Prepared." A reputation for excellence and integrity is most helpful. A reputation is something that you can't buy and that you can't retrieve if lost. It is to be developed and cultivated. Luck and grace are important to success. But be prepared to recognize grace at your door; be prepared for those moments of good luck. Only then will you recognize and capitalize upon them. Have strong hobbies and outside interests to balance your life. It is trite but true that all work and no play makes Jack a dull boy. In my case, it is basketball, UCLA athletics, antiques and music. I recommend a healthy dose of spirituality. Whether religion, meditation or the pursuit of a higher calling in some other fashion, it will uplift your daily endeavors and infuse your life with the mystery and appreciation that makes the difficult times easier to bear. Romantic relationships are essential. Find the right person. I admire those who work in isolation, but passion and teamwork begin at home. Eventually, this may lead to a family, and there is nothing that energizes the middle phase of your career more than children. I also heartily recommend charity work: "giving back" to the community, or to those less fortunate, or to those who will follow in your footsteps. Finally, have an appreciation and gratitude for the gifts that God has given you. And, if all else fails, buy a golden retriever.

> —John G. Branca, music lawyer,
> consultant, Board of Trustees, UCLA
> Athletic Department

I haven't changed my style in twenty years . . . and that style is to get mad when things go wrong.

> —Alexander Haig, President,
> United Technologies Corp.,
> former U.S. Secretary of State

What you have to tell yourself is "I'm not a failure. I failed at doing something." There's a difference. I always remembered the words of a crusty female naval officer who was noted for shaking things up. She said, "A ship is safe in port . . . but that's not where a ship was meant to be. Get out there

23

in rough waters." I believe if you're not failing . . . you're not trying anything different. You're not challenging yourself.

—Erma Bombeck, humorist,
syndicated columnist

The real challenges begin as you strive for achievement outside the boundaries of the classroom. As time goes by, you will be called upon to define the meaning of real success. In my capacity as an internationally syndicated newspaper columnist, I have interviewed hundreds and hundreds of famous people who made remarkable achievements in their professions, but, with a focus only on career, ended up bankrupt in terms of the riches that truly count—a close and loving family and caring friends. From their examples I learned that real success transcends professional accomplishments alone. However, that certainly doesn't mean you can't have both. As for professional success: doggedly pursue your dreams in spite of the odds against you. You will find that reaching your goals isn't as difficult as it may seem, because many with similar ambitions will drop out, finding a multitude of excuses for not being able to do what they want to do—rather than simply digging in their heels and doing it.

—Marilyn Beck, syndicated columnist

2

Aim High

Fortunately, I learned early in life that if you work hard and are prepared, when you are called on to perform you will be able to accomplish your goals. It takes a lot of unspectacular preparation to achieve spectacular results.

—Roger Staubach, former NFL
quarterback

As a student you learned to research, forecast, balance time, set goals, tolerate pressure, and compete with your peers. Now you have to utilize those valuable skills, earn a living, and create a career path. How do you accomplish your goals? Merge pride with humility, replace self-doubt with confidence, substitute positive energy for insecurity. Project an at-ease, confident (not arrogant) persona. Temporarily discuss your immediate needs, survey the "big pic-ture" possibilities, and focus on your contributions to your new employer's success. Read articles/books on creating a memorable, success-stamped impression. Participate in role-playing mock interviews. Plan to "dress for success," selecting an interview outfit both reflective of your style, and also in sync with the corporate image. Approach your interview with a sense of adventure and a respect for the employer's needs as well as your own. There are a thousand and one interview tips, but if you do your homework, you will be able to anticipate the standard interview questions. Bottom line—project a smile, a warmth, a focus, a firm handshake, receptive body language, and quick, appropri-ate responses to the interviewer's cues. You are the product and the "packager" of your presentation; and you have a five-to-twenty-minute window to market your assets. Take risks, face your fears, believe that you deserve success. Al-low the "real you" to shine through and you will succeed in making "the right connections."

—Pauline Cymet, President/Cofounder,
Right Connections Entertainment
Personnel Agency

Remember the past, plan for the future . . . but live today. It's important to remember we live—and do our work—in the present. Too many "mañanas" or "there's always tomorrow" help destroy our personal focus with the here and now . . . or the personal time in which we actually exist and accomplish things.

—William J. Avery,
Chairman of the Board/President/CEO,
Crown Cork & Seal Company, Inc.

Don't measure yourself by what you have accomplished, but what you should have accomplished with your ability.

—Ben Chavis, former Executive Director,
NAACP

I started my career when I was sixteen years old, becoming a reporter for the *San Francisco Chronicle,* not long after World War II started in the U.S. Contrary to today, I had only served one high school term learning journalism but I widely expanded my understanding of journalism while working for the *Chronicle.* In later years I worked for *Colliers* magazine, *L'Express,* a French weekly news magazine, fifteen years for ABC News as Paris bureau chief and later chief foreign correspondent. I was able to move up in the journalism world because of my ability to create high-standard, worldwide journalistic sources. Part of this ability came from my government career when I was press secretary to Presidents John F. Kennedy and Lyndon Johnson, and my brief career as United States senator from California. The second part of my ability came from living in Europe for twenty-five years and traveling across the world creating high contacts, not only in Europe, but in the then Communist eastern bloc countries and the Soviet Union, and in the Middle East. If you want a worldwide journalistic career, you have to spend your time expanding your abilities and expanding your sources.

—Pierre Salinger, journalist,
former Press Secretary,
Vice Chairman, Burston-Marsteller

While setting goals is a critical factor in career advancement, remaining flexible is important too. Climbing the career ladder with blinders on could mean missed opportunities and missed options that differ from original goals. It's never too late to explore other interests, even though they may differ from earlier ambitions. Stay open, stay flexible; make sure you're using your talents to the fullest. Along the way, keep in touch with those who have touched your life: your family, your minister or rabbi or spiritual adviser, teachers, coworkers, supervisors from your first jobs, and friends from your school years. Let them know, when the occasion arises, how their influence has meant something special in your life. And be sure to be there for them if a word or a gesture from you would make a difference. Remember who you are and where you came from, and no matter where you go there will be a base for your career. Whether you're in public service, private industry or going solo as an entrepreneur or in a profession, working hard to the best of your abilities will always be significant in achieving success. Along the way, enjoy what you do and the friends that you make. A career you feel good about will bring the happiest years of your life. You can make it happen.

—Ted Stevens, United States Senator,
Alaska

It is amazing what blind loyalty toward a single goal can produce.

—Sam Wyche, NFL head coach,
Tampa Bay Buccaneers

Take it from me, the most important thing you can do for yourself and for your career is to have a goal. Make it realistic, attainable, and not too easy to obtain. Your goal can be changed, wherever you feel it needs to be. Write down your goal on a piece of paper, date it, and look at it often. Tell as many people as you can what your goal is, and how you intend to accomplish it. The more you communicate your goal to others, the more real and concrete it becomes, and the easier it is to attain. If you don't have a goal, you don't know where you are going or how to achieve what you want. Using the analogy of a road map, your goal (the map) tells you how to get there from here. If, for example, you want to become a television broadcaster on a national network, you should start your conversation, when someone asks, "What do you want to do with your life's work?" by saying, "My goal is to become an anchorperson on *60 Minutes, 20/20,* or *Nightline.*" Work hard toward your goal. Never give up, and you will accomplish it. Remember, never give up—Never!

—Dr. Earl L. Mindell, vitamin expert,
author of *The Vitamin Bible*

It's very important that a young person decide on long-term personal goals and then develop and maintain the inner discipline to keep focused on their multi-year objectives. An overriding consideration in any young person's business pursuits should be complete and total commitment to honesty and integrity. Being true to oneself and acting accordingly must be a given in a person's daily life. The ultimate test should be "Can I look in the mirror every morning and feel comfortable with myself?" Although a short-term advantage can sometimes be gained by acting otherwise, over the long run, such a person is almost certain to fall by the wayside.

—Gerald L. Maatman, President/CEO,
Kemper National Insurance Companies

Never let anyone deter you from your goal—*no one!*
—Sugar Ray Leonard, boxing champion

Being a physician is more than a job. It is a profession, an honor, and a responsibility that changes the way one looks at humanity. A physician is a scientist who strives to improve and prolong life, yet must study and accept disease and death. The information available to treat illness is constantly growing, and is propelled by all areas of science, mathematics, psychology and business. The physician is challenged to use these new advances appropriately, while remembering that the ill patient has a spirit that also needs to be nurtured. Memorizing information and mastering techniques is only part of the goal. A physician must also understand the patient's emotional, as well as physical, pain and respond with both science and compassion. If my goal as a physician is to have all my patients live forever, I will fail 100 percent of the time. However, if my goal is to diminish suffering, provide information and support, and improve my patients' quality of life, I can succeed 100 percent of the time. I am proud to have chosen a profession that challenges me intellectually, and allows me at the end of every day (and often nights and weekends) to know that I have significantly helped, or even saved, a life.

—Stuart Kaplan, M.D.,
Doctor of Dermatology

We must all find our true purpose; like Michelangelo, Mozart or Leonardo da Vinci. Each of us must develop a mission in life.

—Michael Jackson, entertainer

It is essential to remember that a goal is the single most important element to success. Whatever goal you select, that goal provides your definition for victory and success. This is not to say that the goal is always as simple as obtaining a diploma or getting an excellent grade. However, the goal is always the base reason which drives the current action. Too often, the articulation of this base reason is unartfully stated as happiness, success, love, etc. Your goal should be in between the broad life reasons and the narrow means to success: e.g., "To achieve happiness and success I wish to spend my life in a career field which I enjoy, I am good at and which can provide an avenue which will engender the respect of my peers. Consequently, I wish to pass this contracts exam in Law School and graduate at the top of my class." The broad goal (as stated above) is not passing the exam or even passing school in the top 1 percent, but to "spend my life in a career field which I enjoy, I am good at and which can provide an avenue which will engender the respect of my peers." Keeping your eye on the goal will not only allow you to have the necessary flexibility in your plans but will actually permit achieving that goal. If you are too focused on the means to success, then all other avenues of approach to the goal are necessarily foreclosed because you have redefined your goal as the means per se (e.g., passing school in the top 1 percent). To actually achieve the goal you must define it, remember it and work for it. Having said that, selection of a worthy goal is harder than you think. The selection criterion for any goal should be articulated in that goal and always adhered to. In such lofty, life-defining decisions there should be no compromise—after all it's your life, only you can live it and you should live it well because you've only got one shot at it. The goal should be something which you enjoy, something which you can take pride in, something which you can be recognized for and something which allows you to give to others. While an end in themselves, these ingredients for the goal will consequently also spell happiness and success.

—Michael Patrick Flanagan,
Member of Congress,
5th District, Illinois

In order to achieve anything in life, we must make a commitment and have a deep conviction that we will relentlessly pursue our goals. We must exercise great discipline and sacrifice in order to find success. We must be sure that the goals and rewards we see in life are worth the price we will have to pay. Success does not come easy. Every single person is a creation of God and has a God-given talent. We must find that talent and then maximize it to the best of our ability. In other words we must be the best we can be.

—Mike Ditka, football great,
NBC sports analyst

3

The Right Stuff

When I was about twelve years old, I came across something in a reading book that I've never forgotten: A "Boy Wanted" ad had been placed in a newspaper, and a dozen young fellows showed up to apply. They sat on a long bench in a narrow hallway, and as each of their names was called for an interview, they rose, stepped over a broom that was partially blocking the hallway, and walked into the employer's office. The last boy, upon encountering the broom, did not step over it, as had all the others, but had the good sense to move it out of the way. Given that all the teenagers were approximately equally qualified, the one who had moved the broom was hired. Your future employers will obviously expect you to do the work for which you were hired, but they will particularly appreciate any exercise of extra energy and common sense. Many of us develop poor work habits during the years of our schooling, not adequately preparing for tests until the last minute, forgetting instruction, failing to hand in homework, etc. You can get away with that in school, but not for long in the marketplace. A third bit of advice concerns the personal image you present to others. The approach to life characteristic of the world of rock music works only in that one field. If you want to hold a regular job, put aside all the freaky looking nose rings, zombie hairdos, bizarre attire, and drug use. Also become aware that English is a beautiful language, and learn to speak it as coherently and grammatically as you can. This means you should be able to communicate simple thoughts without cluttering up every sentence with such goofola interpretations as *you know, like, hey, the whole nine yards,* and the use of the word *goes* for says. You can do nothing more important than to learn to read and write well. Without these basic skills you have an almost insurmountable handicap in your journey through life and in the workplace. I suggest you make use of all the writing resources available to you. You might start by dusting off your grammar and English textbooks from your school days. Become familiar with your local library, which will offer you a bevy of books, as well as videotapes and on-site programs to improve your ability to read and write. Once you've honed these skills, a whole new world will open up to you.

—Steve Allen, comedian, author, actor, composer

Never be frightened by those you assume have more talent than you do, because in the end energy will prevail. My formula is:

Energy plus talent and you are a king.

Energy and no talent and you are still a prince.

Talent and no energy and you are a pauper.

This is even better expressed by Henry Wadsworth Long-fellow, 1807–1882:

"The heights by great men reached and kept

Were not attained by sudden flight,

but they, while their companions slept,

Were toiling upward in the night."

—Jeffrey Archer, politician,

author of *Kane and Abel*

Career success depends an self-discipline, tenacity, literacy, a positive attitude, a desire to fulfill one's potential, and the choice of a career that will inspire enthusiasm, energy, and pleasure. If you form good study and reading habits, establish firm goals and direction, and strive for excellence in everything you do, you will find the career ladder easier to climb. Personal honesty, altruism, fairness, and a sense of compassion, combined with a sound knowledge of your field, will improve your chances for career success. Personal success can be achieved not only in a career that requires advanced education, but in the most menial work, provided you take pride in your performance and the work brings self-satisfaction and a sense of fulfillment.

—Michael E. DeBakey, M.D.,
medical pioneer

I suppose the one quality in an astronaut more powerful than any other is curiosity. They have to get someplace nobody's ever been.

—John Glenn, American astronaut,
United States Senator, Ohio

A career is different from a job. A job is something you go to at 9 A.M. and leave at 5 P.M.—it's a place from which you draw a paycheck. A career has a life of its own. It has vision, a purpose, and grows with you as you accept more responsibility. There are three things that I would suggest in planning a life and career: First, develop personal relationships with your business associates. Second, be creative in whatever you do. And finally, wherever your career may take you, get involved in the community in which you

40

live. Throughout my career I have held that in order to succeed, you must develop personal relationships with your colleagues and your customers. You just can't get things done strictly on a professional basis. You need to have personal contact with people to really have them respond. Socialize with people, perhaps take a vacation together, have dinner with them once in a while. Do whatever is comfortable for you. It is very difficult to succeed professionally without good friends. Be creative throughout your career. Find a special way to showcase your accomplishments. When I was a new salesman in a territory off the beaten path, I negotiated the largest contract in the history of the company. I could have just sent the order in to be processed, but I knew that our president has a special affinity for the company I had just signed to a contract. So, I got a silver platter, placed the order on top of the platter, and had someone deliver it directly to the president. I gave him his favorite company "on a silver platter." That's the kind of thing I am talking about . . . have fun with whatever you are doing. Finally, wherever your career may take you, be sure to get involved in the community. Today people are frequently transferred around the country, and the best way to become acclimated to a new area is to become active in the community. Get involved in your church, serve on the PTA, take an active role in charitable organizations. By helping to enrich your community, you are also enriching yourself. Take it from me—I owe my success to those three simple tasks.

—Don Hastings, Chairman/CEO, the
Lincoln Electric Company

If I could focus some career advice through the fine lens of hindsight, I would offer three principles my parents taught me: work hard, enjoy life's opportunities, give back. When my family lost their home during the Depression, my father salvaged lumber from a burnt-out building and constructed another house for our large family. As a boy, I worked alongside my dad in the vegetable garden that produced much of our food, and later joined him in his trade as a metal lather. He taught me the rewards of self-reliance more by example than by word. And when I became the first person in my family to attend college, my family's faith and confidence in my ability to work sustained me in this intimidating venture. Inherent in this effort, of course, was a sense of purpose. And I grew up knowing that that purpose should reach beyond just the immediate goals of the individual. My parents also encouraged our family to take advantage of life's opportunities, and to approach them with a sense of humor. Despite our relatively meager circumstances, my mother saw that each of her children learned to play a musical instrument. I didn't say well, mind you; but she taught us to look beyond the obvious and be open to the possible. Despite the crushing tragedy in her own life—the untimely deaths of four of her children—my mother continuously looked for ways to help others. And, she taught us to receive graciously as well. If we couldn't return the compassionate act directly, we were to pass along another kindness somewhere else down the line.

—Orrin G. Hatch, United States Senator, Utah

Preparing for That Job Interview: It is mind-boggling how often someone will come to me for a position without knowing a thing about Remington beyond the identity of its chief product. Never enter an interview without having acquired as much information about your prospective employer as possible. For my very first job interview with Lever Brothers, I compiled a dossier on the company that included bios of its key executives and board members; a list of the company's products, especially the more obscure ones; a breakdown of the company's performance over the previous five years; and a profile of its most recent advertising campaigns. Anyone can get such information. Valuable facts fill the pages of trade journals and business magazines. If you are considering a publicly held corporation, you can acquire its latest financial statement or annual report. You should also find out who handles the company's advertising. Call the agency and discover what percentage of your prospective employer's advertising dollar is spent on television, radio, or print media ads. Study those ads to determine which direction the company is taking. For a somewhat dispassionate assessment of a company's strengths and weaknesses, talk to its suppliers and accounts. If you are armed with data, you will control the moment. When I attended that interview at Lever Brothers, I knew so much about the company I was able to ask as many informed questions as my interviewer. As the session wore on, our roles reversed. I became the interrogator. This gave the impression that I was there to make a decision about the company instead of asking it to make one about me. Creating such an atmosphere always works to your advantage. You can hype a questionable product for a little while, but you'll never build an enduring business.

—Victor K. Kiam, CEO,
Remington Products, Inc.

The way I see it, if you want the rainbow, you gotta put up with the rain. If there's one bit of advice I'd give to young people trying to break into show business it would be this: Don't assume that the people on the inside know what in the hell they're doing. He may have a big office and a fancy suit, he may have power to hire you or not, but he probably has no idea whether or not you have any talent. Even if he has an opinion, he probably has to clear it with guys in even bigger offices with even more expensive suits and even less of a clue. There's a joke around Hollywood about a writer who runs into a studio executive over the weekend. "What did you think of the script I turned in on Friday?" the writer asked. The studio executive answers in all seriousness, "I don't know, so far I'm the only one that's read it." Although the ratio may be better than in some other businesses, show business is still essentially a man's world. It can be difficult dealing with that as a woman; it can be very difficult if you're a five-foot-two blond with a hick accent. In addition, every difficulty factor is multiplied by two for every cup size. Being a woman in show business is kinda like being a bird dog in heat. If you stand still they'll [spit at you]; if you run, they'll bite you in the ass. I've learned to use all of that to my advantage. There are basically two kinds of men you have to deal with in business, the ones who want to screw you out of your money and the ones who want to screw you, period. The second guy is the easiest to deal with. If I catch a man who's not looking into my eyes as he talks to me, I've scored two really big points with him already. A smart woman knows that she can take a man that thinks with his small head and quickly turn the would-be screwer into the screwed. Pardon my language, but I have to get this out. I should point out that I'm not interested in screwing anybody . . . professionally . . . I never want more than anything that's fair.

—Dolly Parton, entertainer

I'm a father and grandfather, now about fifty years old. I've worked in a variety of occupations including college professor and coach, typist, house painter, small school administrator, personal fitness coach, and now self-employed professional author, lecturer and business entrepreneur. From this midlife vantage point, I can offer career advice based on the hard-earned wisdom of experience. Advice is a tricky matter, however, so I start with this disclaimer: We may have very different inner drives, motives, talents, and experience. What is true for me may not be true for you. Having said that, here are some of the things I've learned: Few people really know what they want to do until ten years out of high school (or college). We may think we know what we want to do, but we rarely know for certain. Some people, out of a discomfort with uncertainty, settle on something early in life, and climb to the top of their career ladder only to find out it's leaning against the wrong wall. A period of testing, experimenting, trying things out—even uncertainty or instability—can, for many, be natural and beneficial.

Applying the universal principle that "you have to kiss a lot of frogs before you find your prince(ess)," we often spend time finding out what we don't want to do before we settle on what we find especially suitable to our needs and talents. If we were exactly alike, there might be only a few books in the library, and only a few kinds of work. It's for each of us to come to know ourselves, to clarify our values, ambitions, strengths, and weaknesses before we find the most suitable form of work or service in the world. General guidelines: Although nearly every kind of work has its burdens, challenges, and downside, don't do something that conflicts with your deepest values. Don't work at a job that exploits others, and don't allow yourself to be exploited. Find a way to make what you consider good money doing what you enjoy, serving other people. Out of a genuine sense of service, no matter how humble, comes a feeling of pride in your work from which abundance flows naturally. If you're doing something just for the money, you might want to reconsider. There might be no perfect work, but there are forms of work more or less right for you. It takes courage, the willingness to risk, to give up one kind of work and go back to school, get more education or training, or form your own business. There are no real failures, because we learn and grow. Never forget that for all its frustration, challenge, as well as satisfaction and reward, finding and pursuing a career, our form of service in the world, is a path of personal growth.

—Dan Millman, lecturer, author of
Way of the Peaceful Warrior

Everyone has talent. What is rare is the courage to follow the talent to the dark place where it leads.

—Erica Jong, author of *Fear of Flying*

Everybody talks about wanting to change things and help and fix, but ultimately all you can do is fix yourself. And that's a lot. Because if you can fix yourself, it has a ripple effect.

—Rob Reiner, actor/director

I'm an owl. I hope to watch, to learn and be wise. If it ever came to a choice between compromising my moral principles and the performance of my duties, I know I'd go with my moral principles. At this point, I must tell you two of the most important lessons I learned from those and other challenges I have faced: (1) don't dwell on disappointment—determine to do your best anyway, and (2) we don't always know what's best.

—Norman Schwarzkopf, General,
United States Army (Ret.)

Volunteerism has always played a role in American progress. Working together, helping one another and getting involved is the only way we can overcome the mounting human and social problems which beset our nation. Make your life meaningful and productive. You're never too young, so start here and now! Make today the stepping stone to tomorrow. There is no challenge that you cannot meet—you can do it!

> —Ray R. Soden,
>   past Commander-in-Chief,
>   Veterans of Foreign Wars

Integrate what you believe in every single area of your life. Take your heart to work and ask the most and best of everybody else, too. Don't let your special character and values, the secret that you know and no one else does, the truth—don't let that get swallowed up by the great chewing complacency.

> —Meryl Streep, actress

You can use all the quantitative data you can get, but you still have to distrust it and use your own intelligence and judgment.

—Alvin Toffler, author of *Future Shock*

⚬═══✦═══⚬

Be nice to people (especially assistants); tell the truth even if you are scared, and only pick a career that you really love.

—Elizabeth Warner, talent executive,
Buena Vista Television

⚬═══✦═══⚬

The greatest single asset that a person can possess is character—a basic characteristic that is not clearly visible but which is contained in a person and comes out in one's conduct. It is evident by one's actions, one's demeanor, and one's performance. It reflects sincerity, honesty, and selflessness. It abhors lying, cheating, or stealing. It pushes aside a phony. It is real, not artificial. To be successful, one must learn to get along with people, and people are all different but all have common characteristics, take it from me. People expect to be treated with dignity and they don't like to be talked down to. Their pride may not be evident but it is there. People take pride in being a party to a successful project. Nothing succeeds like success and success is a product of sound thinking and hard work. All parties to an endeavor should understand that each played an essential role and are associated with success. Sloppy work is a no-no. Good work is expected and outstanding work should be recognized. The "Boss" must "know his stuff" and be businesslike but not arrogant.

—William C. Westmoreland, General,
United States Army (Ret.)

Career advice is so involved that a few words may do an injustice to the subject. I will try to summarize my thoughts as briefly as possible. (1) Choose an occupation that both thrills and challenges you. If at any point along the way you are disenchanted, then make a change as soon as possible. Bouncing from one job to another too often can be detrimental, but remaining with something you dislike will most certainly ruin your chances for success and happiness. (2) Keep you eyes on the ball and your mind focused. To achieve success, compensation should not be your number-one consideration. Experience has taught me that perfecting my skills, committing all of me to the accomplishments I sought, and engaging my associates to work as a team were my prime objectives. Compensation and other benefits just came along automatically. (3) I hear it often said, "It's not whether you win or lose, it's how you play the game." That's hogwash. Winning is all that counts as long as you win honestly, treat your associates and customers fairly, and practice the best of ethics throughout your career. Compromising good business practices, no matter how tempting, will in the long run lead to failures. Lastly, the opportunities for a successful career have never been greater than they are now. Set your goals very high—your imagination is your only limit.

—Erwin Zaban, Chairman Emeritus,
National Service Industries, Inc.

My advice to the young person looking forward to a career is as follows: Get a well-rounded basic college education. Delay, until you are certain, the decision as to whether or not to specialize beyond that basic education. Plan and strive to work in two or three unrelated occupational areas before selecting a lifelong career. Enter each job with the determination to do your best work. Do not be deflected by pressures to accommodate unprofessional solutions; adopt as your criterion for excellence that you will leave your position rather than to accommodate unethical pressures. Remain loyal to those who serve you well. Help them along on subsequent careers when your paths part.

With regard to your supervisors, keep in mind that the highest form of loyalty is to give them frank and honest advice rather than telling them what they want to hear. Keep fit. The winning of the professional race requires good health and energy as well as intelligence and administrative courage. Do not win by compromising the careers of good people—it will come back to bite you—if not in this world, then in the next. The essence of what I have learned in seventy years of life and adventure is that perseverance and drive are far more important than one's physical or mental capabilities when it comes to both happiness and success in life. To me, the most important model with which to guide one's life is "if at first you don't succeed, try, try, again."

—E. R. Zumwalt, Jr., Admiral,
United States Navy (Ret.)

4

Make It Count

You only have one chance to make a first impression. Make it count.

—Markita Andrews, Girl Scout who holds the record for cookie sales

Abraham Lincoln attended church one Sunday and heard a well-known minister who, many thought, was at the peak of his form because the President of the United States was in the audience. When asked what he thought of the sermon, President Lincoln said, "Since you've asked, I must confess I didn't think much of it." "Why?" he was asked. Lincoln replied, "Because he didn't ask us to do anything *great*." SOME CHALLENGES: Do you care enough about you and your loved ones to put some *muscle* into your dreams? Do you care enough to define *yourself?* Do you care enough to *confront* your hopes? Do you care enough to *ask* much from life? Do you care enough to *build* "for giving" relationships? Do you care enough to *seek* strengths in all things? Do you care enough to replace cynicism with *wonder?* Do you care enough to *eliminate* the apostrophe t's from you vocabulary? Do you care enough to *share* the real you with others? Do you care enough to distinguish between tranquility and *real* happiness. Do you care enough to *lead?* Expect the Best!

—Joe Batten, Chairman of the Board,
The Batten Group

My days in basketball and politics have taught me that hard work, discipline, and concentration are my cornerstones of success and that teamwork is the mortar that holds it all together. Slick moves and an inflated ego will never challenge genuine excellence, or what can be achieved when motivated people pull together.

—Bill Bradley, United States Senator,
New Jersey

You cannot paint the *Mona Lisa* by assigning one dab each to a thousand painters. The more complicated and powerful the job, the more rudimentary the preparation for it. You cultivate the essential virtues: high purpose, intelligence, decency, humility, fear of the Lord, and the passion for freedom.

—William F. Buckley, Jr., syndicated
columnist, political analyst, author of
Up from Liberalism

Motivation, old-fashioned values and self-confidence separate winners from the "all talk and no action" people. Always focus on being number one.

—Joe Girard,
Guiness World Book of Records'
"World's Greatest Salesman"

Whatever your chosen field of endeavor, the difference between a career and a job is your willingness and ability to take responsibility for producing results that make a positive contribution to an organization's goals. Education will provide you with the solid foundation on which to build your career. It will empower you to think strategically and make decisions. This empowerment, combined with ambition, initiative and imagination, is the component you need to produce results. As you progress up the career ladder from team leader to manager of one or more subordinate teams, there is an additional component you will find increasingly valuable to assure the production of positive results. It is the ability to lead, motivate and incentivize each employee to contribute his or her own ambition, initiative and imagination to his or her role in accomplishing the common team goal. It has been my experience that the best way to incentivize team members is through recognizing and rewarding excellence—outstanding individual performance that makes a significant contribution to achieving the team goal. An effective award can be an organization-wide employee recognition program or bonus compensation or both, as we have at Tyco.

—L. Dennis Kozlowski, Chairman/CEO,
Tyco International Ltd.

Don't let bad grades in school, alcohol, drugs, gangs or bad influence keep you from being the best at whatever you choose to do. For me it was basketball. If it's sports for you, terrific! If you want to be the best pianist or musician, great! If you want to be a doctor, go after it!

—Nancy Lieberman-Cline,
women's basketball star

The preparation for tomorrow is to do your best today.
—Lou Gossett, actor

Be the best you can be. Maximize your talents by pushing yourself to your own personal limit as often as possible. In doing so, you will also help others achieve this same objective. All anyone can ask of you is to do your best—the problem is defining exactly what this means. In a highly competitive world, this, for me, means always trying to figure out how to push yourself to the next level of your ability. Some of the ways to achieve this include: Read everything you can get your hands on, always strive to be open-minded, listen, deliver. If you say you are going to do something—*do it*, react in a timely, on-time manner, be

59

disciplined and focused, be a team player, and learn to recognize windows of opportunity. The biggest decision you have to make is how devoted to your career you want to be. Pushing yourself to the limit does not make for a balanced life. The kind of focus required to be your best takes hard work. If, however, a few times in your life you are able to maximize your talent in a particular situation, the reward—the feeling of achievement—is unmatched.

—Jerry Solomon, sports manager

Whatever you do, take your time and do it well. Make all your work a representation of who you are, what matters to you, what makes you special. We are in a historical period of shortcutting, of getting places fast and effortlessly, of looking for angles and not wasting time—and yet we are wasting ourselves in the process, and leaving behind very little that will identify us. Technology is taking over, and unless we assert ourselves we'll be reduced to a microchip, a functionary fraction too small to matter. We must personalize our work, rise above the ordinary and practical, and strike out in new directions with a sense of being unique and singular. And lasting—and eternal.

—Gay Talese, author of
Thy Neighbor's Wife

Spend whatever it takes to build the best. Then let people know about it. In New York, there is no limit to how much money people will spend for the very best, not second best, the very best. Experience taught me a few things. One is to listen to your gut, no matter now good something sounds on paper. The second is that you're generally better off sticking with what you know. And the third is that sometimes your best investments are the ones you don't make.

—Donald Trump, real estate executive

Nobody remembers who came in second. The world is filled with Monday mornings! There are few things in life that are more tragic than to have passed up opportunities that would have given your life complete fulfillment. Many, many people have only weekends and holidays to which they can look forward, leaving the rest of the time dreading having to go to work on Monday morning. Get all of the education possible for you, and set yourself the goals that will bring you the satisfaction that you deserve.

—Charles Schulz, cartoonist

The most powerful advice I ever received, I received from a man who passed away thirty years ago, and it is this: "Do what you do (no matter the job) *so well* that people want to see you do it again and when they do, they will go out and tell others."—Walt Disney.

—Bobbie Gee, speaker, consultant

5

Get Your Priorities in Order

Don't let your schedule determine your priorities, let your priorities determine your schedule.

—Stephen R. Covey, best-selling author of *The Seven Habits of Highly Effective People*

Most people have an overblown view of how many hours they work. It's hard: Working eighty hours is very hard. You can't do much else if you're gonna do that. So there's lots of weeks I work eighty hours, but I think my average is lower than that . . . On average I take every other weekend off . . . I'm probably more like seventy average now. There are some weeks I work more than eighty. Like those weeks I travel to Europe: That's all I'm doing is working, sleeping, working, sleeping. So you can get weeks where I'll put in over ninety. I mean, I assume you don't count reading business magazines, the *Journal* or the *Economist*. When I was in school, I always had a dilemma: did I want to be a scientist; did I want to be a computer programmer; did I want to be an economist? You have to pick; you can't do everything. Although I don't know what those other jobs would have been like, I suppose I might have liked to be a mathematician or to have focused on work with artificial intelligence. I'm a big fan of scientists. [The late Nobel Prize–winning physicist] Richard Feynman is probably my favorite. I like so many things, but I think that I chose the right job for me.

—Bill Gates, Founder, Chairman, and
Chief Executive of Microsoft Corp.

TEN COMMANDMENTS OF BUSINESS

1. Work like hell. Try to do more than what's expected.
2. Smile often and stay in the positive.
3. Read, study, learn everything you can about the field in general and your area in particular.
4. Judge yourself from the position and point of view of your superior.
5. Setbacks are necessary in order to grow. Learn from them.

6. Don't expect to be perfect. Do expect to face your mistakes and don't repeat them.

7. Accumulate good experiences and good business associates. It makes for good references, and you never know when someone will return the favor.

8. Never manifest anger. When you can't control a situation, put it aside until you can deal with it unemotionally. There's nothing wrong with manifesting emotions as long, again, as they're positive.

9. Develop interests outside of the job that you can share with your coworkers or superiors, even it it's only keeping current on good restaurants.

10. Never leave a position of your own volition unless there's somewhere else to go, preferably upward. If you're unhappy or dissatisfied with your job, discreetly look around.

*And my eleventh—Keep sex out of the office unless you work for *Playboy*.

—Marilyn Grabowski, photo editor,
Playboy magazine

Making a success of one's career is almost entirely a matter of hard work, and consistency of purpose, tinged with a little luck. You don't have to be a genius to get to the top but you do have to stick to it, enduring a few ups and downs along the road. It takes time. Plenty of young journalists and writers when talking to me, speak enviously of my position. I immediately remind them that I had not even published a book until I was forty-two years old. I was thirty-six before I landed a staff job on the *London Sunday Times*, and forty-eight before I joined the *Los Angeles Times*. Before then I was just a patient hack, the proverbial fire-engine-chasing reporter, building up experience, waiting to pounce on opportunities, and raising a family without the stress of being at the top. Now, at sixty-five, with fifty years of journalism behind me, and ten books published, I've had a long and satisfying career. If you rush to acquire fame and fortune in your twenties or thirties, and get it, what do you do with the rest of your life? Start at the bottom and keep climbing is my career advice. And, by the way, also enjoy life outside of work to the fullest extent possible.

—Derek Humphry, journalist, author of
Final Exit

I believe that, no matter what career you choose, a lifetime commitment to social activism will introduce you to exciting ideas, a broadening perspective and interesting, well-rounded people. But there is more to social action than voting and taking part in protest, important as they are. My experience has taught me that it should also be a part of our daily lives. In family life, I have found that it means resolving conflict with spouses and children in a nonviolent, mutually beneficial way. I've learned that it means teaching our children the values of concern and compassion for the needy and suffering. On the job, it means reforming the company or employer from the inside and proposing creative policy reforms and community service initiatives. And I feel strongly that it means never letting a bigoted remark by a coworker or business associate go unchallenged and speaking out against injustice whenever it surfaces. I think that, sooner or later, we all come to a fork in the road to personal fulfillment. The well-worn "careerist" path leads to increased material comfort, complacency about social injustice, and the illusion of security. But the other, less-traveled route requires personal sacrifice and humanitarian service. Instead of a false sense of security, it offers a deeper sense of fulfillment based on the recognition of our interdependence. In my experience, this is the road to true wholeness.

—Coretta Scott King, Chair/President/CEO,
the King Center

To run life's race we need to be fit. Fitness of mind and body, over which you have a great deal of control, should be one of your lifelong top priorities. Health should always come ahead of wealth. When it does, you'll have the energy and drive to reach your goals—then financial security will follow. Eat right, exercise regularly and get plenty of rest—that's a simple regimen for good health. Faith is the starting point for all accomplishments in life. The power of strong desire backed by faith is incredible. We conquer fear with faith. The absence of faith is a guarantee of failure. If you believe you can do it—you can!

—Walter Payton, retired football star,
President, Walter Payton, Inc.

Don't be afraid to take risks. If your every move is calculated to be risk-free, you're not going to succeed at work . . . or in life. Work for tough bosses when you get a chance, and learn everything you can from them—even if it's how not to treat people. Be alert, and be a voracious reader of a variety of material, whether it's on paper or on-line. If you allow your focus to become too narrow, you will have single-handedly undermined your opportunities to go beyond middle management—and to fully enjoy life. Listen. Have fun . . . because it helps you keep your balance. Cultivate self-discipline and initiative. There will be hello's and good-bye's. There will be ups and downs. You will determine their outcome. Make your commitments to enduring values and institutions—honesty, integrity, trust, confidence, family and other matters of the heart. Go ahead and challenge the status quo, but you must also decide what lasts—what really counts—what no one can take away from you. These are your values, and they will accompany you wherever you work and wherever you live.

—Jack D. Rehm, Chairman/CEO,
Meredith Corporation

The most important task to consider during the months before graduation is not developing a targeted résumé; and it's not rehearsing the interview dialogue you expect will occur. While those are very important tasks that will help differentiate you from the masses, they should not be your primary concern. Your first objective should be to interview yourself, beginning with the hardest questions—What do you think you want to do in life? What do you like to do and why? What are you truly good at doing and why? This will be the hardest interview you'll face. Your answers may even surprise you. The outcome, however, will provide you with something invaluable—something thousands of other college grads won't have—a recognizable focus and direction in your life that will translate to prospective employers through the substance of your résumé and in the answers to even the toughest interview questions. I was fortunate enough to find these answers early in life. Achieving a focus and direction in my life provided the groundwork for succeeding in graduate school and in a career that has included federal government service and award-winning work in advertising and marketing communications. It has also provided the necessary foundation for achieving balance between quality time spent with my family, significant involvement in community service and dedication to my work.

—William L. Ussery III,
Manager, Communications,
Mercedes-Benz of North America, Inc.

The management techniques I applied in building Domino's Pizza were developed mostly by trial and error. But all of them were based on homemade philosophy I call my five personal priorities. My five priorities are spiritual, social, mental, physical, and financial, in that order:

Spiritual—My background makes concern about spiritual matters as natural to me as breathing. My religious faith is strong. I know I would not have been able to build Domino's without the strength I gained from my religious faith. When it comes to secular matters of business, my spiritual priority is expressed in the Golden Rule: Do unto others as you would have others do unto you.

Social—A loving wife and family are, to me, essential for a happy, productive life. After family on my scale of social relationships comes friends. Nobody can succeed in business without the help of friends.

Mental—Factor in maintaining a healthy mind and a clear conscience. This means you have done your best to live up to your own expectations. A clear conscience fosters self-esteem, a positive attitude, and an optimistic outlook, all of which promise success in business.

Physical—It may sound corny, but I subscribe to the idea that the body is the temple of the soul. If I lost my health, I'd give every penny I had to get it back, and I don't know anyone who wouldn't.

Financial—The financial priority is last on my list because it arises from the others. I know that if I attend to the first four properly, financial success will follow. Another important principle I've stressed over the years is Have fun in the work you do. I believe that if you've chosen the career that is right for you, it will give your life a feeling of purpose.

> —Thomas S. Monaghan,
> Founder/Chairman,
> Domino's Pizza, Inc.

Advice for young writers is always, unfailingly, no matter what, even under threat of death, write honestly. Never try to guess what it is people want from you. Write what it is you absolutely believe in. That's the only thing that is worth it.

> —Bob Guccioni, Jr., Editor, *Spin* magazine

There is something sick about a person whose only interest is money. And the same can be said, I think, for the company whose sole goal is profit.

—Robert Haayen, Chairman,
Allstate Insurance Co.

There is only one thought to be concerned with—is it legal—and will it make me happy? Well, those are two thoughts, which brings us to thought number three—there are a lot of thoughts involved, but the goal should be happiness.

—Buddy Hackett, comedian

During the course of my business career, I had many colleagues come to me and lament their not spending more time with their family. One said, "My daughter, her husband, and their new baby are moving back to Columbus." I replied that this would give him a chance to know his new grandson. Then he said, "Yes, but it'll also give me a chance to get to know my daughter. I was too busy when she was growing up." Balance . . . that's the one word I want you to remember! You work to live; not live to work. Keep a balance in your life . . . a balance between work and family . . . a balance in everything you do.

—James K. Baker, CEO,
Arvin Industries, Inc.

6

Take the Lead

Effort brings success. Whatever career you choose, your best efforts to gain knowledge and experience will give you an advantage that others will lack. The simple truth is success is earned. Doing a job right—no matter what it is, no matter how small it seems—is education that isn't going to be forgotten. There always will be leaders and followers, but leaders don't start at the top, they learn and work their way there. They see opportunities in their jobs, and are rewarded with promotions. That's important to remember: Leadership is learned. It begins by doing small jobs well, so that the individual is ready for the next step—to learn a new job, to take on more responsibilities, to be promoted and to grow as a person. When I started Wendy's, I saw that opportunity of having a few restaurants. When they were built, we saw other possibilities, and the company grew, and still more opportunities opened up. None of them knocked, but they were all around us. Look, and you'll see them, too. My first employers taught me the importance of being polite and of praising people for a job well done. When you work hard and apply yourself, you succeed. It's really not that complicated.

—R. David Thomas, Senior Chairman/
Founder, Wendy's International, Inc.

I don't set trends. I just find out what they are and I exploit them.

—Dick Clark, music industry executive

Management by objectives works if you know the objectives. Ninety percent of the time you don't. To improve communications, work not on the utterer, but the recipient. People who don't take risks generally make about two big mistakes a year. People who do take risks generally make about two big mistakes a year.

—Peter Drucker, American business
philosopher

I'll tell you what makes a great manager: a great manager has a knack for making ballplayers think they are better than they think they are. He forces you to have a good opinion of yourself. He lets you know he believes in you. He makes you get more out of yourself. And once you learn how good you really are, you never settle for playing anything else than your very best.

—Reggie Jackson,
former baseball player,
New York Yankees

Good organizations have leaders at all levels and they nurture them. Learn all that you can from these leaders, by working with them and watching them in action. Here are three lessons I have learned by doing just that: The first lesson is that an effective leader sets the vision, the level of expectation. In other words, a leader has to state where—and how far—the organization is going and have a plan for taking it there. The second lesson is that a leader has to involve people in the process. A leader cannot simply say "believe me"—he or she has to install the values in others, and make them believe, too. Finally, the third lesson is that a leader must encourage leadership—and create an atmosphere where leadership is accepted and, in turn, risk is encouraged. What difference does effective leadership make? For business, the most obvious indicator is a healthier bottom line. But good leaders enrich the performance and culture of the organization and the lives of its people by building pride and a sense of purpose and accomplishment. They are personally driven to achieve much more than they ever thought possible.

—William F. Patient, Chairman/CEO, the
Geon Company

For men and women interested in public service, law enforcement can be rewarding in the fact you are responsible for the safety and well-being of the community where you may be employed. It is not as portrayed in movies or television with blazing firearms. Your duty is to prevent crime and act as required to enforce the laws. Your power comes from the people who trust you to carry out your duties fairly and to make decisions under your own discretion. Be prepared to assist those in need; use your powers of police authority with understanding and tolerance. There is a great sense of satisfaction to this position and with constant training and desire you may become a leader in law enforcement as well as a protector of life and property.

—Joseph McCaffrey, President,
American Federation of Police

If I had to sum up in one word what makes a good manager, I'd say decisiveness. You can use the fanciest computers to gather the numbers, but in the end you have to set a time-table and act. And I don't mean rashly. I'm sometimes described as a flamboyant leader and a hip-shooter, a fly-by-the-seat-of-the-pants operator. But if that were true, I could never have been successful in this business. I have found that in order to become successful, you must determine what you want, and then be willing to work tirelessly to reach your goal. The people I know who have become successful have done just that. The best advice I can give you is to get a good education; it'll help prepare you for whatever career you choose. I have found that being honest is the best technique I can use. Right up front, tell people what you're trying to accomplish and what you're willing to sacrifice to accomplish it. People say to me: "You are a roaring success. How did you do it?" I go back to what my parents taught me. Apply yourself. Get all the education you can, but then, by God, do something. Don't make excuses. Don't just stand there, make something happen.

—Lee A. Iacocca, former automobile
manufacturing executive,
Ford Motor Co.

A little uncertainty is good for everything. The task of the leader is to get his people from where they are to where they have not been.

—Henry Kissinger, former United States
Secretary of State

7

Dare to Dream

Stay involved. Reminiscing is great, providing it's linked to the future. An older person needs a dream as well as a memory.

> —Arthur S. Flemming, former Secretary of
> Health, Education, and Welfare

Believe anything is possible and you can do it.
> —Wendy Kopp, President,
> Teach for America

Have a bias for action! Don't overanalyze. Don't hesitate while looking for the perfect result. Do it. Correct, aim later. You may not see the real target until later. I wish you the very best career and a fulfilling career. The world is changing very rapidly. The years go by so fast. Don't hesitate. Get started next Monday. When in doubt—believe in your intuition—envision your dream.

—Earl E. Bakken, Founder/Director,
Medtronic

The best career advice I can give you would be to start in an area you enjoy and you are interested in. Then, educate yourself as much as you can in that area—both in the written word and through practical experience, if possible. Next, make a clear written plan of what you'd like to be doing and what you'd like to achieve in this area. In other words, what would it "look" like if you were successfully achieving in this area on a day-to-day basis. Then, finally, just go for it without reservation. Be passionate, centered, honest, and keep your word!

—Cathy Lee Crosby, actress

Careful self-evaluation will lead you to appropriate avenues for your talents and ambitions. The journey will involve no more than the qualities we have discussed—initiative, discipline, curiosity, creativity, diligence and vision. By doing your best, striving to grow and serve to the extent of your ability, you can travel light-years from the humblest beginning. So set your sights high; the world is full of opportunities for service and anxious to make use of your talents.

—Lodwrick M. Cook, Chairman/CEO, ARCO

If one is lucky, a solitary fantasy can totally transform one million realities.

—Maya Angelou, poet, author of
I Know Why the Caged Bird Sings

Dare to dream! Dare to hope! Dare to see yourself as a great big bundle of potential. Psychiatrists are increasingly acknowledging the value of daydreams. Studies have shown that people who have the highest IQs tend to spend a lot of time daydreaming—imaging how things could be. Most of the truly great inventions and developments of history started out as images in the minds of dreamers. But remember, a dream is only a dream until you make it come true. Ralph Waldo Emerson was one of the greatest visionaries of history. Yet Emerson said to an aspiring artist, "There is no way to success in our art but to take off you coat, grind paint, and work like a digger on the railroad, all day, every day." Either you dream of bigger and better things, or you fall into the pit described by Henry David Thoreau when he said, "The mass of men lead lives of quiet desperation." Obviously, the practical side of dreaming is being willing to pay the price to make those dreams come true. Many people are not willing to pay the price to become successful. Each day presents us with a wide array of possibilities and potentialities. Opportunities parade before us like the stars on a cloudless night. Seize the moment—dream big dreams—work hard to accomplish them—and live life more fully and purposefully forever.

—Nido R. Qubein, Chairman, Creative
Services, Inc., professional speaker

You've already learned much about what it takes to be successful in school. It's much the same no matter what school you're attending or what work you're doing. To me, what makes someone successful is managing a healthy combination of wishing and doing. Wishing doesn't make anything happen, but it certainly can be the start of some important happenings. What makes the difference between wishing and realizing our dreams? Lot of things, of course, but the main one, I think, is whether we link our wishes to our hopes and our hopes to our active striving. It might take months or years for a wish to come true, but it's far more likely to happen when you care so much about it that you'll do all you can to make it happen. Wishes are sometimes grand and far beyond the reality of the present, but other wishes are intimate. They're about simple things of daily life expressed again and again in our contacts with other persons around us. I trust that you'll feel good enough about yourself that you continue to wish and dream. And that you'll do all you can to help the best of your wishes come true.

—Fred Rogers, host of TV's
Mister Rogers' Neighborhood

I do *not* believe we are all born equal. Physical and emotional differences, parental guidelines, varying environments, being in the right place at the right time, all play a role in enhancing or limiting an individual's development. But, I *do* believe every man and woman, if given the opportunity and encouragement to recognize their potential, regardless of background, has the freedom to choose in our world. Will an individual be a taker or a giver in life? Will that person be satisfied merely to exist or seek a meaningful purpose? Will he or she dare to dream the impossible dream?

—Hugh O'Brian, actor, Founder,
Hugh O'Brian Youth Foundation

When one is young, the whole world stretches out ahead, beckoning with dreams and hopes. Thanks to spending most of my adult life at the University of Notre Dame, I have known many young people who want their lives to make a difference in the years ahead. Many of them have their doubts about whether or not one person can make a difference. I have always told them: you can make a difference, can help make a better world more just, more peaceful in the years ahead, if you really believe it is possible, if you try.

—Theodore M. Hesburgh, C.S.C., President
Emeritus, University of Notre Dame

Many of the world's great scientists, philosophers, and political leaders started with the courage of their convictions and ended up leading the world into new frontiers of knowledge or accomplishment. Perhaps the most important component of individual success, however, is the ability to inspire others toward accomplishing shared dreams, to enhance individual effort through teamwork. The ability to fully develop and utilize our skills—both as individuals and as members of a team—begins with dedication. The most complex challenge facing our nation's educational institutions and its businesses is preparing our workforce and our workplaces for today's and tomorrow's intensely competitive environment. While I am optimistic that the next decade will be a period of great economic opportunity, there is mounting concern that we will not have the traditional abundant supply of effective workers needed to fuel the growth.

—T. Marshall Hahn, Jr., Chairman/CEO,
Georgia-Pacific Corporation

Write down on paper what you want to be, what will be required to accomplish your plan/dream, the significant milestones you must successfully pass along the way to be on schedule. Why put it on paper? Because that's the only way you will seriously consider the matter and evaluate the alternatives. You should carry it in your wallet and read it every day to remind you where you want to go. Once established, you must then pursue your plan/dream with a dedication and single-mindedness that will carry you over the rough spots. You must have the courage to stay with it. This means you must be willing to make the sacrifices and put forth the work to make your plan a reality. It won't be easy, but the rewards of success are second to none.

—William E. C. Dearden, former Chairman
of the Board, Hershey Foods

8

Do What You Love

Life is change. Don't get stuck in a livelihood that offers you no growth challenges, and has no "gold ring" as an upside. Everyone's first career is an accident. Your second career is your mighty vocation that you must embrace with maximum awareness and commitment. Invoke the power of the god of transitions, Mercury, to find method for your madness by redesigning your life in your own Type C self-image. Go for it!

—Kenneth Atchity, producer,
literary manager

The best counsel I can offer people is to choose a profession that they really like before spending a lot of time and money studying or training for it. I would also suggest that if a person finds their chosen work interesting and fun, then they shouldn't be too concerned about salary. I'll give you an example: When I was in journalism there were four or five very talented students in my class. After graduation they had a choice of either working for Associated Press at a very meager salary or becoming public relations people for Southern California Gas, which paid terrific salaries. The students who chose the gas company all admit they wasted their talent. Those who began on the wire services achieved considerable success and were much happier about their careers. One more thought: You have to have fire in your belly to get anywhere. I know very few people who achieved their goals without really having that feeling. Finally, people should assume that the person in charge of giving them a job is an idiot—but is always treated with respect. The farther you get away from Washington, D.C., the more you think that things are under control here.

—Art Buchwald, writer/humorist

I have produced eight children. I have tried to teach them to be passionate about their interests and follow them enthusiastically and doggedly. They all share my enthusiasm for life. They also use failure as a learning ground.

—Woody Fraser, television producer

Scanners are people who want to taste everything. They love to learn about the structure of a flower and they love to learn about the theory of music. The great poet Robert Frost defined scanners very neatly when he said, "A scholar is someone who sticks to something. A poet is someone who uses whatever sticks to him." Career aptitude tests tend to miss scanners.

—Barbara Sher,
best-selling co-author of *Wishcraft*

The most important task one must deal with in preparing for a career is to make sure you know what line of work you want to be involved in. I believe the more serious problem that young people face is that they try to make a career in an area that they haven't truly studied and researched to see that they have (a) the background, (b) the talent, and

91

(c) the likability of their chosen career. I believe that people should take off approximately two years between high school and college to have time to seriously deal with what they'd like their future to be. Most of the workers in America wake up after ten or fifteen years in a given area or profession to find out that they're very unhappy. They're bored and really don't see any future in what they're doing. This in turn invites the kind of frustration that drives people to try and change their life work when it's too late. Assuming that you do know exactly what you want to do, then I would say it's the old-fashioned adage of hard work, being prepared, and most of all, needing a lot of luck. You can't settle for a door that is closed. There is always a way to get your foot in it.

—Bud Yorkin, television executive

Find something you enjoy, work hard at it, and as soon as the division, company, dream or whatever starts to come to fruition and grow, go on out and find good people who share the enthusiasm, create the atmosphere to keep them and let them do their job.

—Thomas C. Sullivan,
Chairman, RPM, Inc.

Do What You Love and the Money Will Follow is the title of a best-seller written in 1987 and is the best advice I can offer. A recent poll showed that nearly 90 percent of all Americans do not enjoy the work they do. If it's "only a job" then our relationship to work is tantamount to clock watching and robs our companies and ourselves of energy and satisfaction while we live a life of "quiet desperation." I eat, breathe and sleep PLY GEM. I am the single largest shareholder and it encompasses all aspects of my life. As CEO, one of my most important roles is to provide leadership and create an environment that motivates ordinary people to do extraordinary things. Determine what your real abilities are and what career best suits your personality. Then, give more than 100 percent commitment to achieving your goals. Education and life experience are important, but it is determination and perseverance that gets you to the top. And remember, it's not where you start but where you finish!

—Jeffrey S. Silverman, Chairman/CEO,
PLY GEM Industries, Inc.

My career advice: Ask yourself the following questions, and write down the answers: What do I love to do? What do other people say I'm really good at? If I had a million dollars, but by law I still had to work, what job or career would I do? What do I see as my unique skills and abilities? Once you've reflected on the answers to those questions, take some time to slow down and contact your intuition. Ask your intuition (or Higher Self), "What do I need to know to take the next step in fulfillment and prosperity in my career?" Then, listen for any feeling, image, or realization that feels right to you. If nothing occurs to you right away, be on the lookout for the answer coming to you during the next couple of days. The quickest way to not have to work for a living is to do work which excites you. If you're doing what you love, then you're not really working for a living. If you don't like what you're doing now, take small, but consistent steps that will allow you to transition to a career more suitable to you. Each person has a unique destiny. Your mission, should you decide to accept it, is to discover what your unique contribution to the world is. When you're aligned with your mission, you'll feel lit up like a light bulb.

—Jonathan Robinson, psychotherapist,
workshop leader, speaker

In the last twenty years, I have spoken to groups of every size, age and mix throughout the United States, Canada, Australia and New Zealand. Due to the nature of my topic, people often share with me their disappointing career paths. So often, they have entered into a field in which they have no interest or aptitude. Their career choices had been made for them by a well-meaning advisor or parent. They were stuck trying to be what their father never was or what their mother wanted to be. Once I share with them that as adults they must make their own choices, many men and women leave jobs they hate to discover new and more personally rewarding work in an area which suits their own personality style, interest level and area of gifting. My ultimate advice for anyone starting out in the professional world or in a place of making a change is know who you are, what your skills and interests are, and pursue your own dream, not the dream of others!

—Florence Littauer,
President, CLASS Speakers, Inc.,
author, lecturer

The best thing you have to offer the world is yourself. You don't have to copy anyone else. If you do, you're second best. To achieve success is to be first and that's being yourself. After high school I went on to Texas Tech with the intention of becoming an architect. But I quit to become a singer. Not one person said I was doing the right thing. Everyone said I was making a big mistake. They even turned me down for the shows at Six Flags, and I wound up handling the little cars the kids drive. But I knew deep down inside I was born to sing for people. And singing is the most joyful thing in the world for me. It's what's inside you that counts. And if it's not what you want to do, don't do it. Listen to yourself. You'll always know what's right. Listen to that voice. That's how you find success as a human being. Don't be afraid to be who you are. It's not that tough.

—John Denver, singer

Find the work you love most and do it with a passion. The result of this decision will certainly mean that there will be no such thing as work . . . each day you'll be going to life.

—Leo F. Buscaglia, Ph.D.,
author of *Love*

You can be born with $100 million, but unless you find something you really enjoy, the money is of no consequence. I believe that you're OK if you do something you like. I always did something I would do for nothing.

—David Brown, film producer

You can be born with $100 million, but unless you find
something you really enjoy, the money is of no
consequence. I've always gone by the rule; if what I'm doing
in my life isn't enjoyable, I would rather not
be doing it in the first place.

9

Beyond the "Three Rs"

Amateurs hope. Professionals work. Maturing men and women must avoid ruts, fixed habits, old ways. The antidote to changing is action, both physical and mental, and learning. Life is not, or should not be, a spectator sport. It must be lived, not just observed.

—Garson Kanin, playwright, director,
author of *Hollywood* and *Moviola*

Find a mentor in your field. Choose someone who is older than you. Someone you look up to and respect. Meet with your mentor regularly. Ask questions. Listen, listen, listen, listen and listen. Take notes. When you do talk, ask more often than tell. Then listen again. If you are a young man in the professional speaking business and you're not being admired by an older man, find one. If you're a young woman in the professional speaking business and you're not being admired by an older woman, find one. Keep looking until you find the right one. A mentor will take ten years off your learning curve.

—Chuck Moorman, Director,
Institute for Personal Power

Use your school years not just to amass raw knowledge, but also to learn how to analyze, organize, and plan. Once you are with an organization, and it doesn't matter whether it is very small, very large, or somewhere in between, learn all you can about its history, what it does, how it works. Try to understand what your boss, and the managers up the line, are trying to accomplish. This will help you become more effective in supporting them. If there is a longtime employee who is willing to answer your questions, take advantage of his or her experience. The step beyond understanding your organization is understanding the external forces that affect it. Every organization has them, whether it's a commercial business, government, education, the military, a charitable group, even a religious organization. Finally, and probably most important, develop a restless dissatisfaction with the status quo. Can something be done better? Can it be done faster? Do we need input from additional people? Do we need to break down the walls of functional "bunkers" that stand in the way of true communications? Armed with open communications and the freedom to act there will be few, if any, challenges you cannot meet successfully.

—Donald R. Beall, CEO,
Rockwell International Corp.

Be willing to serve time as an intern in the office or profession you have chosen. Get all the experience you can get. Then make yourself invaluable to your company. Then ask for a raise.

—June M. Cunniff, executive

I think the most important thing in the world for career and social success is for a person to be well-read. Even if you are not well-read, and most of us aren't, you could read the *New York Times* and the *Wall Street Journal* every day and you'd still be light-years ahead of almost everybody else. I am all for a general excellent education in English, Literature, History, Biography, and the Arts. And this reading education should be ongoing. Today, it seems a firm computer education is a necessity. In my era, I always knew it was important to know how to touch type, and I also have a smattering of shorthand. It is amazing how handy both

these skills have been to me for getting it done and doing
it myself, which is one sure way to get it done. Attitude is
everything in getting ahead. You need to think every minute
and analyze your reactions and behavior. Are you part of
the problem or part of the solution? If you aren't operating
for the latter goal, then you *are* part of the former. People
like me, who got ahead by becoming first-rate second-rate
aides to important people, always have the choice of pre-
senting problems to "the boss" like dead kittens at their feet.
Once I liked the idea of doing that because it seemed like
a kind of fun thing to say to the VIP—"this can't be done"—
I began to forge far ahead myself. Courtesy, common sense,
sensitivity, manners, thoughtfulness, fair play, can all be serious tools to success. They are the oil in the crankcase.
Don't stay in jobs you hate. Success is loving your work. Go
to it!

—Liz Smith, syndicated columnist

If you are interested in getting into sports public relations,
I advise you to do the following: (1) Obtain a strong writing
background. People don't understand that strong writing
skills are a necessity in public relations. I think some students choose a public relations major because they think
all they will do all day is meet and greet people. From writing press releases to story pitch ideas, I would say more than
half of this job is writing. (2) Do an internship for little or

no pay. I worked an unpaid, one-year internship with a sports team immediately after college. I learned my way around a pro sports PR office and made a lot of contacts. One of those contacts led me to a full-time position with another organization. (3) Don't expect to be the general manager after your first year with the team. It's hard enough to get in with a sports team and then once you're in, there is virtually no movement since people love their jobs. You have to pay your dues and it may take seven to ten years just to move from an assistant position to a director position. Be patient. (4) If you hate long hours and low pay, don't get into this business. Sports PR can be really fun and, as I like to say, better than a "real job." Since you work long hours, your fellow employees will become some of your best friends. I wouldn't trade my career for anything.

> —Joyce Szymanski, Director of Public
> Relations, Harlem Globetrotters
> International, Inc.

Don't just learn something from every experience, learn something positive.

> —Allen N. Neuharth,
> Founder, *USA Today*

Study. Learn from the wise. Look to those who are doing what you would like to do, and figure out what it is that they are doing that makes them successful.

—Wesley Snipes, actor

For starters, know your stuff. Study hard at your chosen profession. Master its skills. Today's working world is an intensely competitive place, and knowledge is the basic price of admission. Think and compete globally. Markets, capital, technology, information and products increasingly ignore national borders. You need to learn about other cultures—how they think, how they communicate, how they do business. A second language is good; a third better. Be flexible but durable. The world is changing; don't let it change without you. The ability to learn, adapt and absorb the inevitable failures is key to staying in the race. Know how to lead. Leadership is more than authority; it's courage, vision, ethics and a grounding in reality as well. Think about leadership. Read about it. Study it in the leaders you respect. It's important. And remember, none of this works without determination. Success is not for the ambivalent. It's for those who know what they want and go after it, no matter how difficult the path.

—Alex Trotman, Chairman/CEO,
Ford Motor Company

Today, just having a college degree is not enough. Economic unpredictability demands agility at all levels. Agile professionals, those who pack their résumés with skills that adapt to the economic environment's changing demands, are the ones who will stand out from the crowd. Learn to type: According to the February 1995 Gibbs Report, a survey of one hundred Human Resources executives at Fortune 500 companies, 87 percent still test applicants' typing skills. Graduates quickly discover how important typing skills are in the screening of applicants. Many times, the first question asked at an interview for an entry-level job is "How fast can you type?" Technology is the key: The more office technology you know, especially computer software packages, the more marketable you will be. As technology advances, computers have become essential to the business world. Companies are looking for job candidates who are already proficient in the software programs they use. Have a professional attitude: According to a 1994 survey by the Census Bureau, attitude ranks as the number one factor used in making hiring decisions. An interview situation is your chance to show the interviewer how you will act on the job. Never underestimate the importance of appropriate dress, posture, eye contact and facial expression. Gain business experience: Working at a summer job or internship will provide you with valuable hands-on experience in the business world. Experience, especially in your chosen field, will demonstrate your interest in the field and establish that you are able to function in a business environment. Know your strengths and weaknesses: But, be

105

sure to present all information in a positive light. Sell your capabilities as a prospective employee and address how you will help the company grow. Many graduates are discouraged at the thought of having to take an entry-level administrative position, but this is often a good place to start. Entry-level employees are taking on a much more important role in the workplace than they have in the past, and once an entry-level staffer is in place, good work is likely to be rewarded. Don't be afraid to make a good impression on the ground floor!

—Eleanor P. Vreeland, Chairman,
Katherine Gibbs School, Inc.

The three Rs—reading, 'riting and 'rithmetic—are no longer enough. We must add the three Cs—computing, critical thinking, capacity for change.

—Fred Gluck, former Managing Director,
McKinsey & Co.

If I went back to college again, I'd concentrate on two areas: learning to write and to speak before an audience. Nothing in life has more impact than the ability to communicate effectively. I can't stress enough how important this period of time is in life. By forming good morals and learning the meaning of right and wrong, you form a pattern that will follow you throughout life. I encourage you to set goals and strive for excellence in all you do. The experience, knowledge, and discipline you acquire during your youth is of immeasurable benefit in your adult life and how you affect this nation and its people.

—Gerald R. Ford, former President of
the United States

I'm sometimes asked which high school class did me the most practical good. After much thought, I realized that the most honest answer was: The summer-school class I took in typing. In the age of computers, typing is a skill even more useful than before. If you cannot type, you cannot interface usefully with a computer, and will be at the mercy of those who can.

—Roger Ebert, film critic

The first thing you need to do is establish an interest in the career you want to follow. One way, of course, is through education, taking courses that show aptitude and interest. It does not mean you have to take journalism courses. Political science, English, economics and other liberal arts courses might be an even better route because you get a better all-round education. But you must establish through work on the high school and college newspapers or weekly or daily newspapers (via internships) that you clearly have an interest in the field. Too many students/graduates decide upon graduation that they want to be journalists. That's really a little late because others have made a mark during high school and their years in college. So get moving in the right direction early.

—John J. Curley, Chairman/President/CEO, Gannett Co., Inc.

"Life is made up of sobs, smiles, and sniffles, with sniffles predominating." O. Henry said these words many, many years ago. Those words are as true today as they were the day he said them. "Life is not fair, and the sooner we realize this, the sooner we can get through life's hurdles." We repeatedly hear over and over again the ingredients of a good school. It is not about how many children are in the classroom, or what kind of background the children come from. But it is about the teacher that stands before that class, and what is taught in the school. It is about children learning to think critically and analytically and a teacher bright enough to keep them interested and motivated. Yes, it is about the teacher who becomes more excited each day about teaching. And yes, finally, the good teacher teaches as if their very lives depended on it, and it is about what is "caught" by the children rather than what is "taught" by the teacher. It is this kind of teacher that gives might to the American dream. It is this kind of teacher that takes a lump of coal and makes it a shining diamond.

—Marva N. Collins, educator

If learning is the key to full freedom in America, it must necessarily be true also that people must be free to learn. I had an astonishing experience in Brooklyn. I met at Brooklyn College with several hundred young students there and young volunteers in community service programs all across the country. And we heard presentations from nine people who painted a stark portrait of America as it is: A wonderful woman from Detroit whose two sons had been shot down in a gang fight, one of them dying, who channeled her heartbreak into building a program, the acronym of which is SOSAD, to try to give young people the chance to avoid the fate that her son met. We met with a young teenager from Oakland, California, who had been caught in a crossfire and had his body shattered. He lost an eye. He was paralyzed from his waist down. One of his legs had been amputated. He was confined to a wheelchair. And do you

109

know, he is spending his life telling people who are the victims of violence, of gunshot wounds and knife wounds, not to be full of vengeance and bitterness, and trying to convince them and their families not to shoot back, not to stab back, not to fight back, but instead to build back their lives. This young man riveted that crowd. There were many others who came there, a young man from New Jersey who left a corporate career in New York and instead took his necktie off and put a T-shirt on and decided to devote the rest of his life to building one-on-one relationships with kids in trouble, to give them a chance to get to the point where they would be free to learn. You can teach the illiterate to read. You can teach the frustrated to be peaceful. You can raise the children up when they are very young. You can help to implant values into children who aren't getting them in other places. You have a larger, a different, a more profound mission than ever before.

—Bill Clinton, 42nd President of the
United States

In your very early work years concentrate on what I call the essential infrastructure skill: writing. Like it or not, the written word is still the coin of the realm in information exchange. You can be the smartest financial expert, the most knowledgeable systems engineer, a brilliant scientist. However, if you can't communicate through writing you will not advance. So, every chance you get, instead of calling someone and leaving a voice message, put your thoughts in writing and send a fax, letter, or e-mail. Find a writing style you are at ease with. Test and test again that what you write is easily understood by those who read it. You don't have to become Hemingway or Poe. You only have to develop enough skills so that when people read your ideas and thoughts, they not only understand them, they believe them. This is not hard to do. Take a few business writing classes. Read the *Wall Street Journal.* Write letters to editors. Write concise memos to higher-ups. Try to remember that people don't really buy an idea; they buy the expression of the idea.

> —Alan N. Canton, author of *Computer Money: Making Serious Dollars in High-Tech Consulting*

10

If at First You Don't Succeed . . .

If you're knocked down, you can't lose your guts. You need to play with supreme confidence or else you'll lose again, and then losing becomes a habit. I've always preached to our players to have respect for their opponents. There is no victory so sweet as one over a formidable foe, an opponent who has tested our every resource before reluctantly bowing.

—Joe Paterno, Penn State University
football coach

My advice is simple and something that, if followed, rarely fails: the three Ps . . . Patience, Persistence and Perseverance.

—Paul D. Cloverdell,
United States Senator, Georgia

Be tenacious—don't let anyone tell you it can't be done.
—Ricki Lake, talk show host

Nothing succeeds like persistence. The common denominator of all successful people is their persistence. We will all face obstacles on our way to our goal. The key is to keep going, to assess what the next step is, clear away anything in the way of taking that step, and then take it. And if you trip or fall, get up and get going. It's always next and next with as much enthusiasm as you can muster, because the enthusiasm will propel you in the direction you want to go.
—John-Roger, author, lecturer

If there is one common denominator in the biographies of men and women the world calls successful it is this: They get up when they fall down. We all fall down. Only a comparative few are willing and able, again and again, to pick themselves up, dust themselves off and keep on keeping on. This is not to say that all men are otherwise "equal." They are not. The "all men created equal" thesis has misled us; it's simply not true. In your own family, members demonstrate different aptitudes. Environment and heredity have been similar, yet some individuals, within the same family, are better able to solve problems. There are other factors which can contribute to individual accomplishment: health, perseverance toward a single goal, an extraordinarily compatible marriage partnership . . . But I am convinced there is no power on earth which can keep a first-class man down—or hold a fourth-class man up. And that one controllable factor in success is that those who deserve . . . get up when they fall down. I've never seen a monument erected to a pessimist.

—Paul Harvey, ABC Radio news
commentator

Webster's dictionary says an entrepreneur is one who assumes responsibility for an enterprise. What Webster doesn't tell you is this is one of the toughest things you will ever do. People will line up to tell you your idea won't work and why. If what other people think is important . . . don't read any further. To succeed you need to believe passionately and be prepared to overcome all the obstacles that life will throw at you. You will be challenged on every level—emotionally, physically and financially. "Act as if" says it all. If you look like, sound like and visualize your success, you will come to know anything is possible. I used to visualize cosmetics coming off a conveyer belt with my name on the label. I could actually see the compacts being packed into boxes for shipment. I knew it would happen and I never took no for an answer. I learned from each failure and those failures became part of my success story that I knew I would tell one day. I never looked back but remained focused on my future. My future is here. Read your own success story and it will happen.

—Victoria Jackson, Founder, Victoria
Jackson Cosmetics

Success tends to go not to the person who is error-free, because he also tends to be risk-averse. Rather it goes to the person who recognizes that life is pretty much a percentage business. It isn't making mistakes that's critical; it's correcting them and getting on with the principal task. From time to time, look back. Look back and see if you are leaving footprints, and more, if you like where they are going. And, see if you too, with your own hands, can help to make a small piece of America better. Above all, don't be blown by the winds. A world of dramatic change, as our world surely is, is still underpinned by the timeless values of faith, family, honor and community.

—Donald Rumsfeld,
pharmaceutical executive, former
United States Secretary of Defense

Suffice it to say that I have learned, through the grace of God, to roll with the punches and not worry about what other people think. I am, above all, a survivor.

—Elizabeth Taylor, Academy Award–
winning actress

My advice would be: Always remember that in order to achieve all of your dreams, you must be willing to rest little, work much and give up much more. Moreover, never forget that when it seems you have lost a battle, you have not lost the war. Perseverance is the key to success.

—Ileana Ros-Lehtinen, Member of
Congress, 18th District, Florida

You don't concentrate on risks. You concentrate on results. No risk is too great to prevent the necessary job from getting done. I never quit . . . even when the evidence indicated that I should!

—Charles E. Yeager, retired test pilot,
United States Air Force

The truest lesson any successful person can give someone eager for direction: Hang in there. You must try hard, and it's nice—sometimes essential—that you have talent. But if you don't hang in there, you'll never be in a position to capitalize on such things as whimsy, timing, or the inexorable march of time when they affect your own life.

—Rick Telander, senior writer,
Sports Illustrated

Recent grads should know the difference between persistence and pushiness when job-hunting or starting a new job. Employers (except possibly employers of salespeople) are put off by young people with overly "gung-ho" attitudes. Prospective employers are busy themselves and will *not* appreciate daily phone calls from the same person asking if positions are available or if the decision was made regarding a position for which the candidate was interviewed. Likewise, the recently hired will accomplish more through deference and willingness to learn than by offering too many unsolicited suggestions or ideas for "doing things differently."

—Edith Sachs, Public Relations Account
Executive, Stern & Associates

Just never give up; never look back if you want to reach your goals. Profit can be gained from the "down" to reach the "ups."

—Johnny Rutherford, race car driver

If you believe in an idea, and if you believe that the idea should make sense for a particular customer, go back again. I can't tell you how many times I've seen an idea bear fruit when it is presented again at a more auspicious moment. The simple movement of a clock, the flipping of a calendar, can totally alter the dynamics of a selling situation and the receptivity of the buyer. Shortly after Bob Anderson became president of Rockwell International, I suggested that he hire our company to produce an internal promotional film in which Anderson would visit various Rockwell sites and explain their role in the overall operation of the company. We had done this kind of thing before, and we knew it was an effective device for promoting a family feeling in multinational companies separated by great geographical distances. "Mark," Anderson said, "I just took over this job from the man whose name is still on the door of this company. The last thing *I* should be doing now is commissioning a promotional film—but try me again in five years." Almost exactly five years later, I did just that. And Rockwell is considering a commitment of the necessary funds. People are known as much by the quality of their failures as by the quality of their successes.

—Mark H. McCormack, attorney,
businessman

ㅇ━━━⊱━━━ㅇ

It anything is worth trying at all, it's worth trying at least ten times.

—Art Linkletter, television personality

ㅇ━━━⊱━━━ㅇ

I was once asked what I believe is the most important ingredient of success. My answer? Perseverance. The best career advice I can give anyone is to be willing to take risks. That means, be willing to risk failing. Those who don't try, who don't undertake the unfamiliar and confront the unknown, will never fail. Nor will they ever succeed. Every successful person experiences setbacks. But it is how one uses those setbacks that determines ultimate success. The one characteristic shared by those who succeed is the ability to pick themselves up after they've lost a round, and try again.

—Kay Bailey Hutchison,
United States Senator, Texas

ㅇ━━━⊱━━━ㅇ

Persistence separates the great from the average. This was passed on to me early in life and has been my own personal motto ever since. It has seen me through some very trying times as a representative.

—Peter Geren, Member of Congress,
12th District, Texas

Never take anything for granted but do not give up just because certain gifts have not been bestowed upon you either. By developing your natural talents and making a commitment to success, you can easily make up for any advantages that may not have been handed to you. Once you have your first taste of success, you will enjoy it and find it easier to work harder for more.

—Bonnie Blair, U.S. Olympic speed
skating champion

11

The Attitude Quotient

Your attitude, not your aptitude, will determine your altitude.

> —Zig Ziglar, best-selling author of
> *See You at the Top*

Action is the antidote to despair. You don't get to choose how you're going to die. Or when. You can only decide how you're going to live. Now.

> —Joan Baez, singer

Because all of my life I have been involved in comedy, I think I might pass on a little advice that seemed to help me. If you're thinking of doing stand-up, this is my advice: Make up your mind immediately as to what your attitude will be and do only that material that is in that attitude. Also, be consistent with that attitude. Do not change it—believe in it. Curiosity will do more for you in comedy than you can imagine. One of the most brilliant comedians is Buddy Hackett. I have seen him get curious about anything he touches or sees, and from the curiosity come up with a hilarious routine. And above all, do not resort to vulgarity or profanity—it's a cheap way of getting a laugh. That's my advice, and in the words of my wonderful wife—"Take it or leave it."

—Joey Bishop, comedian

You may think that the pursuit of happiness is a very frivolous task to recommend to you in the cloudy world of today. But I suggest we look for the symptoms of our world disorder in the individual. If you consider the personalities of the great tyrants of this century, it will be plain. I think that they were unhappy people, above all embittered and envious; and in their supposed dedication to the vague mass of mankind, they revealed an apathy or contempt toward the worth of any one man. It will, I think, become irritatingly plain to you as the years go by that people unhappy in their private lives are a great liability as citizens, for they have little energy or benevolence left over from their enmities and anxieties to begrudge to other people around them. As you go into your future, find time to become a happy person.

—Alistair Cooke, correspondent,
broadcaster

Commitment can create its own confirmation. To the man who dares not love, the entire world seems barren and dull, the future pregnant with doom. It is love and faith that infuse ideas with life and fire.

—George Gilder, author of
Wealth and Poverty

We need not limit ourselves to one role. We need not allow anyone to build walls for us, and we certainly must not construct them for ourselves. More people need more hope than help. Keep hope alive.

—Reverend Jesse Jackson, minister,
politician

Taking care of your career these days means managing perpetual motion. Your organization will keep reshaping itself, shifting and flexing to fit our rapidly changing world. That's the only way it can hope to survive in this fiercely competitive environment. Look for it to restructure, outsource, downsize, subcontract, and form new alliances. You also can expect flexible ways of working. Duties will be constantly realigned. Short-lived assignments will be common. Maybe you'll work on a contract basis, or spend time on several project teams. You might even end up working for more than one "employer" at a time. You'll probably have a constantly new set of coworkers, more new bosses, even new careers. You're not going to like some of this. Chances are, nobody will like it all. But that's neither here nor there. Question is, will you get the program anyhow? You need to know that resistance to change is almost always a dead-end street. The career opportunities come when you align immediately with new organizational needs and realities. When you're light on your feet. When you show high capacity for adjustment. Organizations want people who adapt—fast—not those who resist or psychologically "unplug." Granted, change can be painful. When it damages careers, emotions such as grief, anger, and depression come naturally, making it hard for people to "buy in" and be productive. But being a quick-change artist can build your reputation, while resisting change can ruin it. Mobility, not mourning, makes you a valuable member of the group. Shoot for rapid recovery. Instant alignment. Take personal responsibility for adapting to change, just like you would if you accepted a new job with a new employer.

—Price Pritchett, Ph.D., author of
The Employee Handbook of New Work
Habits for a Radically Changing World
(© copyright 1994 by Price Pritchett;
Mr. Pritchett is located in Dallas, Texas)

Listen to everybody. Don't believe anybody. Never take no for an answer! Don't let anybody tell you that you can't do it. Whatever "it" is. Know so firmly that you *can* do it, that you are not influenced by all the negativity you will encounter. No one knows anything about what you can do, better than you do. And you can do *anything* you think you can do. Surround yourself *only* with people who are supportive and who make you feel that you can do it. Listen to them. Learn from them. Then *do* it. And enjoy doing it. Until it's time for you to help others know that *they* can do it.

—Henry Jaglom, writer/director,
Rainbow Film Company

Being an entrepreneur is not just long hours and hard work—it's guts. You have to go at it with sheer determination. Otherwise, the pitfalls will put you off. That's why big companies have to go out and acquire smaller ones. There is a quality in starting a business that only an entrepreneur can provide.

—Jeno F. Paulucci, Chairman,
Paulucci Enterprises

I always try to keep in perspective the fact that notwithstanding how daunting our problems are, they are minor and easy compared with people who live with severe illnesses or physical disabilities, or don't have enough to eat or are victims of war or dictatorship.

—Leigh Steinberg, sports attorney

The great pleasure you bring to others reminds me what my dear mother shared: "Humor is the universal solvent against the abrasive elements of life." It is a great adventure and it will continue to be so—I know I will just keep learning and growing until they throw me in the hole!

—Alan K. Simpson,
United States Senator, Wyoming

128

Even though I came from a very poor background and received little encouragement toward goals from family, friends and peers, I am proof that a positive self-image paired with a positive attitude can work wonders.

—Chi Chi Rodriguez, professional golfer

My old football coach used to say, "Saturday, read your press clippings. Sunday, believe them. But Monday show up ready for the game as if no one knows your name, as if you have one game to make your reputation."

—Jack Welch, Chairman, General Electric

I have always believed that AQ (Attitude Quotient) is much more important than IQ (Intelligence Quotient). Always remember that attitude will determine your altitude!

—Kay Yow, women's basketball coach,
North Carolina State University

No matter how cynical you become, it's never enough to keep up.

> —Lily Tomlin, comedienne, star of *The Search for Signs of Intelligent Life in the Universe* by Jane Wagner

I once hired a young woman with a Harvard M.B.A. and a B.A. from another prestigious Ivy League school. An attractive and personable young woman, she expressed inspired enthusiasm at the interview, passed her audition of writing reader's reports with flying colors, and appeared to be the perfect candidate. Although she had no direct experience in the entertainment business, I told her that because I was a risk-taker, I would take a risk on her. I hired her a step up from an entry level position, with an elevated salary, and I told her it was a sink-or-swim proposition. I fully expected her to succeed. Two months later, I fired her. She broke some very cardinal rules with me. She'd asked for a week off after working for less than a month, she whined about wanting a bigger office, she lied to me (in fact, she hadn't written the brilliant reader's reports), she gossiped about me behind my back, and she didn't follow my directions. It was clear, after a few weeks, that she was miserable. She resented doing what she thought was the grunt work and was focused, instead, on how she was going to skip the critical steps to get to the top more quickly. When I expressed my concern to this woman, her response was "But it's *your* fault!" My hardworking assistant, who'd put in twice the hours and had produced well beyond the call of duty, turned to me and said, "I would do anything to have the opportunity that you've given her." Guess who has a better chance of succeeding? There's a lot to learn reading career advice from this one woman's mistake, and it's a mistake I've seen over and over again, particularly in the younger generation. Just because you have the Ivy league pedigree doesn't mean a thing. In fact, you think you've arrived, but guess what? You never arrive. Having career success is a lifelong journey. And believe me, the mountains only get higher and harder. For those with true ambition it's clear that the work is never done. Here are some simple and very effective rules for getting along and ahead, rules which I wish that young woman had learned. Regan's 15 Career Rules: (1) Do your homework. There is no such thing as faking it, at least not for very long. There is no substitute for having knowledge. The more you know, the better equipped you are to do the job. (2) Do more than is expected of you . . . and then some. The young woman I fired was more concerned with using my free movie screening tickets and party invitations than she was in going home at night and searching high and low for good potential projects. Meanwhile, I wasn't using the tickets because I was home every night searching for the next big project. (3) It's hard to find these days, but if you work for an honorable person, you owe them. If you are truly loyal, a good person will reward you. (4) Manners! Manners! Manners! Every truly

131

powerful person I have ever known has impeccable manners. That doesn't mean they aren't killer deal makers, either. (5) Tenacity, yes. Annoyance, no. The young woman I fired once read that I claimed that my tenacity, in large part, resulted in my success. While I often used my imagination to create new ways to solve problems and to achieve my goals, I *never* did it by annoying people. (6) Earn it, don't expect it. So many people want to get there so fast, they arrogantly make demands without earning the right to. You can make demands when you've earned the right to. (7) Again, wanting it all now can ruin your chances of getting it at all. You also have to have patience when it comes to negotiating. If you act too quickly or imprudently, you can ruin your deals. (8) Take responsibility for your actions. You will earn respect if you can admit your mistakes. (9) Next, don't dwell on mishaps, lost deals or bad experiences. There's only one direction to move in and that's forward. Know when to let go. (10) Make a fair deal. Consider the needs of your company, your boss, even your opponent. Think always of the big picture. Make a deal that's constructive to all. Don't try to exploit anyone, as it will come back to hurt you in one way or another. (11) No whining! Whiners are not winners. (12) Create a strategy. Don't react. Make a plan of action that does not involve your emotions. You can not always get what you want and may have to accept it. However, if you've earned the right, you may create a plan which will result in a victory for you. (13) Humor, a must. Life is full of heartbreak and disappointment, so having a sense of humor will make the journey a better one. (14) Balance. Work isn't everything. Having a family, friends, a spiritual dimension, physical care of your body and a sense of community will balance your life and inform your work. (15) Moral courage. Last, but certainly not least, all of your personal and professional decisions should be informed by your moral sentiments. Although at times it seems we are living in an amoral world, exercise moral courage in the actions you take. Making the right choice may not result in your instant gratification, but over a lifetime, you will see that you will gain more, much more, in the long run.

—Judith Regan, President,
the Regan Company (adapted from
The Art of War for Women)

I watch people who let a headache ruin their day. Things like a flat tire, busy phone lines, and crying babies give some people ulcers. Marital spats, financial troubles, and canceled flights give people high blood pressure. But I have to tell you. To me those things are no big deal. I'm just happy to be here!

—John F. Northcott, World War II POW

One of the things that has kept me sane in Hollywood for thirty years is playing sports, so my advice to young people starting out in show business usually comes in the form of a sports metaphor. When a batter comes up to the plate with two outs and the bases are loaded and you're playing outfield, you can say to yourself, "Please God, don't hit it to me." You have to look right at the batter and say, "Please, buddy, hit it right at me. I'm waiting right here. I'll catch it." Then if he hits it to you you're prepared to catch it and you probably will. That's the same attitude that you have to have in show business. You can't just sit at home being scared and wait for the phone to ring. You can't let people see that you are afraid when way deep down inside you are scared to death. You have to be secure and confident in your abilities even before you actually have the abilities to get the job. Half the battle in Hollywood is convincing people in power that you can do a job even if you're not quite sure of that fact yourself. Nobody wants to hire a risk; they want someone they feel is a sure thing.

—Garry K. Marshall, producer/director

1. Life is all about attitude! It is *not* the situation you find yourself in that can destroy you, it is your attitude toward the situation that will either make or break you. A positive attitude will always make you a winner! Never, ever give up!

2. Dare to dream! Without a dream you will never accomplish anything worthwhile in life! You must have dreams and goals, no matter what your age.

3. Learn to live in *forgiveness*! Unforgiveness only hurts *you*! It does not hurt the person you are angry at. Unforgiveness will rob you of joy and peace and creativity. Let it go!

4. Be a giver, not a taker! The Bible says it is more blessed to give than to receive. Try it for yourself and see. It really works. Happy people are giving people!

5. If you can't say something nice about someone, don't say anything at all! Remember the kindest words are often the ones left unspoken!

6. Learn to live "one day at a time"! Yesterday is *gone*, there is nothing we can do about what happened yesterday. Live today to its fullest. Tomorrow may not come. Make big plans for tomorrow but make *today* count!

7. Take care of your health!

8. Guard you mind! There is an old saying "garbage in, garbage out!" The Bible says "as a man thinketh in his heart so is he!" We become what we think!

9. Guard your tongue! Think before you speak! Remember, words can *never* be taken back once spoken.

10. Find God and you will never be alone. Allow Him to become your best friend!

> —Tammy Faye Messner, ex-wife of
> evangelist Jim Bakker

I was dramatically shaped by my grandmother and my aunts, because they convinced me there was always a cookie available. Deep down inside of me, I'm three years old, I wake up and think, "Out there, there's a cookie." Either it can be baked or it's already been bought, but it's in a jar somewhere . . . and so that means when you open up the cupboard and the cookie isn't there I don't say, "Gee there's no cookie." I say, "I wonder where it is?"

—Newt Gingrich, Speaker of the House

I learned that the only real handicaps are those mental and emotional ones that prevent us from participating fully in life. The day my mother made me start dealing with not having arms was the day she gave me wings.

—John P. Foppe, inspirational speaker

Successful people are people who do things that other people are not willing to do. I, too, feel successful people have an attitude that they "get" to work hard, they "get" to do things. With that positive attitude they have the energy that races them past others that are quacking and complaining about what they "have to" do. If you aren't your own best friend, who will be?

—Kenneth H. Blanchard, Chairman,
Blanchard Training and Development,
Inc.

To break this cycle of cynicism, we should adopt the philosophy of "Eagle Excellence" to develop the steadfast character that gives a business, a family and a nation its purpose and pride. To do this we should embrace the eagle in our mind.

—James H. Amos, Jr., Chief Operating
Officer, the Brice Group

12

Listen with the Heart

Sometimes it pays not to follow advice. In 1963, my husband and I invested our life savings in Mary Kay Cosmetics. A month later, he died, and I was told by my attorney and other advisers to liquidate the company in hopes of salvaging some of the investment. Instead of quitting, I pressed on. Later, my accountant told me I was paying too much in commission. I couldn't succeed without reducing our pay scale. Again, I failed to heed the advice and eventually built one of America's largest cosmetic companies. If you think you can, you can. And if you think you can't, you're right. At Mary Kay Cosmetics, we try to instill confidence in women by raising them to success one small achievement at a time, urging them on to greater success. Sandwich every bit of criticism between two heavy layers of praise. I have always believed that "when God closes a door, He always opens a window."

—Mary Kay Ash, entrepreneur,
Founder, Mary Kay Cosmetics

The poet Robert Penn Warren once told me that careerism was death. More than any other life advice, his startling words have stuck with me. If we pursue only what is outwardly expected of us, if we pursue only for financial reward, we doom our lives and keep our souls from work which "inly" rewards and "rejoices," as Emerson would say.

—Ken Burns, television producer,
The Civil War

I'm proud of some of the things I've done and ashamed of some of the things I've done. But, in the midst of it all, God has been at work in my life. He continues to be at work in my life. That's enough for me.

—Sandi Patti, Grammy Award–winning
gospel vocalist

There is no such thing as a career—all you get are present moments. Create within yourself a knowing that there are two of you present at all times. One of you is the witness to all you observe—this witness is unseen, boundaryless, formless and eternal. It is the noticer, observing everything. The second you is that which you the noticer notices. It is your body, your occupations, your ethnicity. Yes, your career. It is your false self in that it would convince you that you are really that which you notice. You are here for a grand heroic mission, and you will know what that mission is if you ignore your false self and go within to listen to that hidden, higher voice. Your purpose has something to do with serving. The only thing you can do with your life is give it away. Therefore, you will find inspiration in your life, not by focusing on yourself and meeting your own quotas, but by fulfilling the quotas of others. Whatever is your bliss will inspire you. Inspire means In Spirit. Do that in this service to others and the universe will handle the details, and surely your career is nothing more than a detail.

> —Wayne W. Dyer, psychologist, radio and
> television personality, author of *Your
> Erroneous Zones*

I address you on the subject of career selection from the standpoint of someone that has had four different careers in the course of my lifetime: business executive (CEO), World War II aviation gunnery officer, United States senator, and international trade consultant and foundation CEO, training a new generation of Lebanon. My advice to you is to choose a career, whether it be business, politics, entertainment, sports, international affairs, medicine, health care, or you name it, that you find most stimulating and exciting and still at the same time would yield to you an income that would be sufficient to support you, your family, and your joint aspirations and hopes for the future. But whatever you choose as a professional field, I would hope that you would do several other things simultaneously. First and most importantly, devote yourselves to a close relationship with God and your family, and this will enrich your life in a way that you cannot now imagine. Devote yourselves to friends, your community and nation in such a way as to also help enrich their quality of life. Whatever your vocation is, an avocation in public life is so important it deserves your attention. Even volunteering to help candidates at the local, state, or national level is always a way to help but also to learn the political process from the bottom up. It would be well also to find a PVO (private volunteer organization) in a field of great interest to you and find a way in which you can be helpful. Much of the work of the United States, for instance, is done and accomplished through organizations. I have found that working with children through Save the Children, working with the elderly through many different organizations during my lifetime, and with the handicapped, which started by volunteering to read books for the blind that I recorded on tape so that they may listen to them, has been satisfying and rewarding. The very fact that you are reading this book, *Take It from Me*, is evidence that you are ready for the road to success. I congratulate you and know that God will bless you in every noble undertaking that you pursue.

—Charles H. Percy, President,
Charles Percy & Associates, Inc.

I know it takes storms in life to perfect us. I also know that I'm not perfected. But I'm glad to know that God loves me enough to stand by me when the storms come! He is faithful.

—Ricky Skaggs, country singer

The biggest people with the biggest ideas can be shot down by the smallest people with the smallest minds. Think big anyway. People favor underdogs but always follow top dogs. Fight for some underdogs anyway. What you spend years building may be destroyed overnight. Build anyway. Give the world the best you've got and you'll get kicked in the teeth. Give the world the best you've got anyway. Failure is never final and success is never-ending. Success is a journey, not a destination. Talk about a blueprint for success. We should all be so firm in our decisions to where we're going, who we are following, and where we will end up. Surely, at best, life is difficult—it was never meant to be easy. So we've been given the commandments for our own good, peace, and comfort. God created each and every person with a special gift. It is up to us to discover our potential and turn those obstacles into opportunities!

—Robert H. Schuller, minister, author of
Power Thoughts

The best advice I can give is that one should try to listen to advice, not with the mind, but with the heart. It has often been remarked that we have an "inner self" or "higher soul" and it is this intuitive, spiritual agent that should be the final arbiter for decisions. In other words, the "gut" response. This is especially true of the actor whose professional life follows no predetermined or easily recognizable path. In most professions there is a linear progression up a clearly defined career ladder, usually from the mail room to the board room. No such comforting predictability awaits the actor, whose career can seem arbitrary and almost accidental. "A pipe for fortune's finger," to use Shakespeare's phrase. The actor has to face a bewildering multiplicity of choices. This is when basic instinct—not an agent, tossed coins, or astrological advice—provides the best guidance. Because acting is more and more a freelance profession, the need for its practitioners to believe that they will succeed, entirely and unequivocally, is paramount. "This above all, to thine own self be true" is one of the best pieces of advice, also enshrined in *Hamlet*, that mirror held up to the nature of the actors' craft that also admonishes, most wisely of all, that "the *readiness* is all."

—Michael York, actor

Put God first, and try to be the best person that you can be. When you do that, there is nothing you can't accomplish.

—Karyn White, singer

Think of your career as your ministry. Make your work an expression of love in service to mankind. Within the worldly illusion, we all have different jobs. Some of us are artists, some of us are businesspeople, some of us are scientists, etc. But in the real world that lies beyond all this, we all have the same job: to minister to human hearts. All of us are here as ministers of God. God can use the flimsiest résumé. He can use the smallest gifts. Whatever our gift is to God, however humble it may seem, He can turn it into a mighty work on His behalf. Our greatest gift to Him is our devotion. From that point of power, doors open. Careers blossom. We heal, and the world around us heals. Stop fighting the world and start loving it instead.

—Marianne Williamson, author of
Return to Love

I was brought up in the Great Depression in a mill town that lost its manufacturing base at the end of the Second World War. My father was an honest man but afflicted with Hodgkin's disease and was too ill to spend much time with me. Hence, with a working mother and an older sister I was pretty much left to myself. As an honor student (I skipped the fifth grade and had an 87 percent average), I guess I was on my way to a career in education or law or medicine or even, God forbid, politics. But on his deathbed my father gave me an edict. He called me to his side and said, (and remember we never had more than a half dozen short dialogues in my entire life), "God gave you a voice, you must sing!" He died that night. While it hasn't been a grand and great glory road, I followed his orders and life has been more than kind. I imagine what I would like to say is that one has got to set his or her sights on a goal and then put all higher energies into attaining that goal. You can only do your best and then pray that Dad and God are pleased.

—Robert Goulet, singer

Everything that ever happened to me of any consequence came about as a result of turning my will and my life over to the care of God as I understand him.

—Ray Conniff, composer/musician

13

Rules to Live By

Don't feel sorry for yourself.

—Mark Hampton, interior decorator

⊙══✦══⊙

The best way to cope with change is to help create it.

—Robert Dole, United States Senator,
Kansas

⊙══✦══⊙

Don't write when you are angry. Through my lifetime, I have found that it is best to sit on something for at least twenty-four hours when you have been angry, and usually you feel differently about it. In fact, a secretary of mine who recently

149

retired used to hold letters that I wrote when I was in that situation and a couple of days later come back and say, "Are you sure you want to send this?" and usually I was in total agreement with her.

—Russell A. Boss, President/CEO,
A.T. Cross Company

Always be ready so that when opportunity presents itself, it won't pass you by.

—Karen Finney, Deputy Press Secretary to
Hillary Rodham Clinton

College grads should consider a career in manufacturing. Companies are unleashing the creativity of workers, putting them in charge of factories that resemble a *Star Wars* set. Teams of workers are practically running small businesses on the factory floor, earning $500,000 and more along with great benefits.

—Jerry Jasinowski, President, National
Association of Manufacturers

Always thank people—*in writing*. Yes, in writing. (E-mail is okay, though still less acceptable than a handwritten note, even in this era of the Internet.) If someone has been kind enough to meet with you in person—to offer career advice, say, or just to discuss your favorite project—follow a day or two later with a short, thoughtful note. Do the same if someone has been particularly generous with his or her phone time. Or if they have agreed to prepare a reference letter for you. Even if someone has done no more than recommend you for a job, such a deed should entitle that individual to a sweet/funny/anecdotal/entertaining thank-you note from your hand. Believe me, this matters. There is so little follow-up in the workaday world that any evidence of your self-discipline and your skills as a communicator will not be overlooked. In fact, it never hurts to write two notes—just to emphasize the point that you are persistent and organized and appreciative. Managing a career is, in part, about managing your image. You might as well help burnish that image by letting key people know that you are thinking about them . . . which, in turn, will cause them to think (at least momentarily) about you.

—Cable Neuhaus, writer, Los Angeles
Bureau, *Entertainment Weekly* magazine

Have some type of position, job, or responsibility, paid, unpaid, credit or none. It doesn't matter, just get some experience. Résumés: Initially, your résumé is going to be viewed for fifteen to thirty seconds, so make it easy on the eye. Grad school: Record numbers of people are going, but should you? Maybe not. You may price yourself out of the market with an unnecessary additional degree. Creativity (on the job): Your ability to be creative is proportionate to the number of ideas you generate. Good, bad, or indifferent, come up with as many as possible. Job-related gossip: Don't do it. If it's supposed to remain in the company, keep it there. If a client tells you something, keep their trust and don't tell everyone you know.

—Bradley G. Richardson, author of
Jobsmarts for Twentysomethings

Make the most of every situation—take on projects no one else wants, and make them winners.

—Alison Stewart, anchor, *MTVnews*

I advise you to keep your overhead down, avoid a major drug habit, and play every day.

> —James Taylor, singer/songwriter
> (from commencement address given
> at Berkeley College of Music)

Noise does no good; goodness doesn't make noise.

> —Brigette Bardot, actress

You've got to be hungry.

> —Les Brown, motivational speaker,
> talk show host

The Top Ten List for Having the Career You Want

(1) Don't trust anybody. (2) Don't make appointments to get a job, just walk in the door unannounced and politely demand to see the head of the company. (3) People who say they are your friends, aren't. (4) Women don't help other women. (5) Don't sleep with anybody to get ahead.

(6) Always double-check to make sure something you have delegated is done. (7) Promote yourself inside your company as well as outside. (8) Always expect to win. (9) Join the right organizations for your field. (10) Never give up. But realize ultimately that the quality of your life and happiness is more important than any job.

—Sue Cameron, author

I think it is very important to know that promptness is all-important to your future employer. Tardiness is inexcusable in my mind. If I can get to work on time so can my employees. Enthusiasm for what you are doing is important too. I don't think you can say, "I wasn't hired to do this or that." If somebody asks you to do something beyond what you think you are expected to do, just do it and show your willingness to be part of the team. Finally, never ever get involved in office politics. Don't gossip about your fellow employees. Don't let everybody draw you into taking sides. They will wind up best friends and you'll end up out of a job.

—Eileen O. Ford, President,
Ford Models, Inc.

In the business world, everyone is paid in two coins: cash and experience. Take the experience first; the cash will come later.

—Harold S. Geneen, Chairman,
ITT Corporation

c=◆=⊃

No one can be right all of the time, but it helps to be right most of the time.

—Robert Half, Personnel Recruiting
Executive, Founder, Robert Half
International

c=◆=⊃

Never, under any circumstance, allow yourself to be treated like dirt by your employers. If any employer discovers that you can be abused or demeaned within the office environment, then your life on the job will be a skein of misery and pain. If your employer cannot treat you even with a token amount of respect, start looking for work elsewhere—no job is worth suffering for.

—Phil Hall, President, Open City
Communications, Inc.

c=◆=⊃

Hit problems head-on. As a general rule, the more uncomfortable one feels with a given situation, the more one should deal with that situation straightaway.

—Arthur B. Laffer, economist

The longer the title, the less important the job.

—George McGovern, politician

Life is to be lived. If you have to support yourself, you had bloody well better find some way that is going to be interesting. And you don't do that by sitting around wondering about yourself. Without discipline, there is no life at all.

—Katharine Hepburn, actress

Don't assume you're always going to be understood. I wrote in a column that one should put a cup of liquid in the cavity of a turkey when roasting it. Someone wrote me that "the turkey tasted great, but the plastic cup melted." So now I say: "Pour a cup . . ."

—Heloise, syndicated columnist

156

There is no such thing as a free lunch.

—Milton Friedman, economist

In any great organization it is far safer to be wrong with the majority than right alone. Be reasonably prepared.

—John Kenneth Galbraith, diplomat,
economist

Remember, slow catastrophes pass quite quickly, too.

—Karl Lagerfeld, fashion designer

The desk is a dangerous place from which to watch the world.

—John LeCarre, British diplomat, author
of *The Spy Who Came in from the Cold*

157

Treat employees like partners, and they act like partners.
> —Fred Allen, Chairman, Pitney-Bowes
> Company

The thing women have got to learn is that nobody gives you power. You just take it.
> —Roseanne, comedienne

This too shall pass.
> —Kitty Carlisle Hart, Chairwoman,
> New York State Council on the Arts

Watch which laws you break.
> —Heidi Fleiss, convicted madame

Learn to write. Never mind the damn statistics. If you like statistics, become a CPA.

> —Jim Murray, sportscaster, writer

If you see a snake, just kill it—don't appoint a committee on snakes.

> —H. Ross Perot, entrepreneur,
> politician

A lot of people will urge you to put some money in a bank, and in fact—within reason—this is very good advice. But don't go overboard. Remember, what you are doing is giving your money to someone else to hold on to, and I think that it is worth keeping in mind that the businessmen who run banks are so worried about holding on to things that they put little chains on all their pens.

> —Miss Piggy, Muppet/entertainer

Rule 1: The customer is always right. Rule 2: If the customer is ever wrong, reread Rule 1.

—Stew Leonard, American merchant

If you expect someone else to guide you, you'll be lost.

—James Earl Jones, actor

Stay away from lawyers. Lawyers are like beavers: They get in the mainstream and dam it up.

—John Naisbitt, author of *Mega-Trends*

Nobody ever drowned in his own sweat.

—Ann Landers, syndicated columnist

In all things keep it simple and foster trust.

—John D. Nichols, Chairman/President/
CEO, Illinois Tool Worlds, Inc.

The rule on staying alive as a forecaster is to give 'em a number or give 'em a date, but never give 'em both at once.

—Jane Bryant Quinn, business writer,
Newsweek

Be aware that any decision you made during your lifetime may find its way onto a television screen.

—Steven Schiff, Member of Congress, 1st
District, New Mexico

Three golden rules of business: (1) Think of something people want. (2) Make it cheap. (3) Sell it a lot.

—Calvert DeForest, a.k.a. Larry "Bud"
Melman, spokesperson

Being the best means overcoming obstacles and giving that little bit extra. That's what separates the champions from the rest. That's true in sports, in business and in life.

—Mary Lou Retton, Olympic gold medalist in gymnastics

I think the one lesson I have learned is that there is no substitute for paying attention.

—Diane Sawyer, newscaster

Have you considered that if you "don't make waves" nobody including you will know that you are alive?

—Theodore Isaac Rubin, psychiatrist, author of *Lisa & David*

If you want something said, ask a man. If you want something done, ask a woman.

—Margaret Thatcher, former Prime Minister of Great Britain

People who fight fire with fire usually end up with ashes.
—Abigail Van Buren, syndicated columnist

I like the way you always manage to state the obvious with a sense of real discovery.
—Gore Vidal, author of *Lincoln*

When you're right you take the bows, and when you're wrong you make the apologies.
—Benjamin Ward, New York City Police Commissioner

Have options. Don't be at the mercy of having only one means of survival. Find other ways and other things to do.
—Billy Dee Williams, actor, artist

Luck is a matter of preparation meeting opportunity.

> —Oprah Winfrey, actress, talk show
> host/producer, *The Oprah Winfrey Show*

Build a house of bricks. Like the Three Little Pigs; not one of wood or straw but of bricks. That's when you don't have to worry about the wolf huffing and puffing and blowing your house down.

> —Steve Wynn, Chairman of the Board of
> Directors, Mirage Resorts, Inc.,
> Las Vegas

Author's Note

A portion of my proceeds for this book will go to the United Negro College Fund.

Founded in 1944, the United Negro College Fund is a consortium of forty-one private, historically black colleges and universities.

Each year, UNCF conducts national appeals to raise general operating funds in support of these institutions, which enroll over 51,000 students.

Perhaps at no other time in history has the importance of the United Negro College Fund work been as great as it is today. Why? Because in the coming years, educated minorities will play a critical role in the effort to keep America growing. The Reverend Dr. Martin Luther King, Jr. is a lasting example of the vision of leadership and potential in these

institutions. With that in mind, I encourage you to give gen-
erously to the United Negro College Fund.

United Negro College Fund, Inc.
500 East 62nd St.
New York, NY 10021
(212) 326-1100

"A mind is a terrible thing to waste."

Talk Back to Michael Levine

Writing a book is a curious experience, much like putting a message in a bottle and tossing it out to sea—you're never quite sure who will see it, when or where.

I've always considered reader feedback vital, and so I encourage you to share your comments with me directly. I'm interested in anything you have to share, but especially interested in learning about your candid reactions to what you read in *Take It From Me*. Feel free to send along a photo, which makes letters significantly more personal.

You can write to me at the address below. I look forward to hearing from you.

Michael Levine
"Take It From Me"
Levine Communications Office, Inc.
433 N. Camden Drive
4th Floor, Suite 120
Beverly Hills, CA 90210

Index

About the Author

Author Michael Levine has been called by the *Hollywood Reporter* "one of Hollywood's brightest and most respected business executives." He heads a prominent entertainment PR firm with offices in Los Angeles, New York, and London, representing top celebrities. Mr. Levine lives in Los Angeles, California.

How to Reach Anyone Who is Anyone

__THE ADDRESS BOOK (7th Edition)
by Michael Levine   0-399-52149-6/$11.00

"The almanac to the inaccessible."—*People*
The definitive guide to reaching just about anyone; provides mailing addresses of over 3,500 VIPs and celebrities in every field imaginable.

__THE KID'S ADDRESS BOOK
by Michael Levine   0-399-51875-4/$9.95

Kids can make a difference, make a suggestion, or make a new pen pal, with more than 2,000 addresses of the most popular and important people and organizations.

Now available in trade paperback...
__TAKE IT FROM ME
by Michael Levine   0-399-52217-4/$12.00

Career advice from the brightest stars in entertainment, business, politics, and sports. From Woody Allen to Donald Trump, the powerful and celebrated share witty anecdotes and words of wisdom on following one's dreams, excelling at work, overcoming setbacks, and reaching the top.